Owen Winter Jr.

The Call: Living Sacramentally, Walking Justly

George McClain, Tilda Norberg, and Nancy Kruh (Editor)
Participant's Guide by Becky Dodson Louter and Pat Hoerth

United
Methodist
Women
FAITH · HOPE · LOVE IN ACTION

TABLE OF CONTENTS

THE CALL: LIVING SACRAMENTALLY AND WALKING JUSTLY

PARTICIPANT'S GUIDE
Becky Dodson Louter and Pat Hoerth

Introduction

By Glory E. Dharmaraj

"The place God calls you to is the place where your deep
gladness and the world's deep hunger meet."
—Frederick Buechner[1]

How do we discern God's call in our lives? How do we respond to our call? How are we enabled to live out our call? What does it mean to cultivate our being—and to cultivate our becoming? This study is an invitation to engage these questions, to deepen our spirituality by experiencing God, and to fully live out our call through a variety of ministries.

The contours of the study delineate, in a variety of ways, how we realize this deep spiritual experience. We will learn how to be open to God's call, as individuals and as members of communities, and how to be perceptive to God's breakthrough moments in our midst. As called persons, we will also learn how to journey inward by cultivating our spirituality and to journey outward by working to make a difference in the lives of others. We will learn, as well, that by living out our calling in a congregational setting, the church can liberate itself from being a mere structure and become a living witness in the world. Moving through the study, we will encounter examples and tools to deepen our spirituality and engage in transformative action.

To set us on this path of "living sacramentally," the study will explore baptism and Holy Communion, the two sacraments that are biblically rooted and affirmed by The United Methodist Church, as well as other Protestant churches.

Writers George McClain and Tilda Norberg will lead us, in Chapter 1, through the meaning and relevance of the sacraments in our changing world. They will grapple with the meaning of grace in the context of the sacraments. The writers include personal illustrations as they address such questions as, how do you live out your baptism? And, how do you stick with the Eucharist even during dry times? They take pains to show that the sacraments are not just relics of the past but also radical events that remind partakers that "God's creation of us isn't over when we are born; it continues throughout our lives. God is there, constantly redeeming and healing and turning things upside down. God even continues to be in sweaty labor to birth the world, panting and pushing to make all things new." Indeed, God's "kin-dom"—the term this study uses to evoke God's egalitarian reign—is already here and not yet.[2]

Baptism, we will find, connects us to the image of God within us, offers us a sign of new life through Christ, calls us to be Christ's followers, and "ordains" us to be in ministry. If baptism provides identity and mission to believers, then Holy Communion offers sustenance, nourishment, and grace for our journey with God. In turn, we dedicate ourselves to be "holy and living sacrifices" to heal a broken world, just as Jesus did through his own sacrifice on the cross (Romans 12:1). The sacraments help us participate in the power of the sacred through the mystery of dying and rising with Christ.

Chapter 2, also written by McClain and Norberg, deals with the importance of keeping the sacramental vision with an understanding of one's individual and collective call to work for God's vision of justice, mercy, and peace for all. The chapter also offers an examination of personal and social holiness.

The writers want us to struggle with how to integrate the personal and the political in our everyday lives. How do we connect our private acts of compassion to the larger context of social justice? To drive home the need for this interrelated approach, McClain and Norberg recall two radically different processions that occurred during Holy Week in Jerusalem: One was an imperial parade of power, might, and wealth by the Roman occupation; the other was a procession of peace, humility, and nonviolent resistance to exploitative power. In this context, the Last Supper takes on a profound meaning. The writers challenge us to reflect on the two processions, along with the story of Jesus savoring Mary and Martha's hospitality, and recognize the interrelatedness of the personal and the political.

Sacramental living calls for courage to stand against multiple oppressive forces and systems that continue to exploit vulnerable people. The writers remind us that, "sacramental living is not for the faint of heart." The mystery of God's presence in the broken bread and the shed blood of Jesus for the redemption of all offers us the strength and sustenance to live out our calling. John Wesley's works of piety—such as Bible study, Holy Communion, praying, fasting, and Christian conferencing and conversation—act as a means of grace for our spiritual growth and feed the roots of transformation.

In this process, the writers caution us to read the Bible with a "critical eye, alert to the reality that enduring truth is often obscured by the unchristlike customs and vocabulary of the times. We should not just question scripture; we should also let scripture question us." The chapter offers helpful tips for engaging in prayer, reading scripture, and Christian conferencing.

In Chapter 3, McClain and Norberg invite readers into a parable, the story of a narrow and mountainous road in need of repair, and how over the years, individuals and groups come up with innovative methods to make it an effective passageway. The needs of people and the promptings of the Spirit lead us to engage in actions that make a difference and address root causes of problems. The writers examine Wesley's understanding of works of mercy, offer examples of how people who have made a difference have lived out their calling, and invite readers to express their own faith through action.

Sacramental living is living daily in the light of God. It is acknowledging the grace of God, seeking inspiration from the life stories of our fellow travelers who have made a difference, and taking a stand for justice in acting out our conversion.

In Chapter 4, writer Nancy Kruh tells selected stories of individuals who have responded to God's call through a variety of ministries. In these stories, readers can hear the voices and experiences of people who have said yes to God's call on their lives. Each story is unique. Each is part of an interlocking web of human responses. An empty nester, a car dealer, United Methodist Women leaders, a home missioner, a deaconess, a violin teacher, a medical student, a retired schoolteacher, a community organizer: each of these storytellers meets the holy and responds to the mystery of call in both ordinary and extraordinary ways.

These stories are intended to expand readers' imaginations, call them to integrate their own life stories, and add more stories, if they choose. At the end of the chapter, Kruh offers a user-friendly tool for anyone interested in collecting stories of call and response in their local church and United Methodist Women organization. Preserving and celebrating such stories adds to the gallery of living witnesses that surrounds us and cheers us on in our individual and communal faith journeys.

Chapter 5, also written by Kruh, reviews the key insights from the previous chapters and helps readers to envision the future that God promises. Readers will be urged to stay focused on God's kin-dom as the prize, while discerning glimpses that affirm God's kin-dom is already present.

In the accompanying Participant's Guide, Becky Louter and Pat Hoerth offer readers liturgical and pedagogical tools to experience the study in a group setting or in individual meditation.

As we prepare our hearts and minds to begin this study, let us first open ourselves to the full awareness that God is calling each of us: individually, insistently, and lovingly. Each of us has an essential role in the world as God's emissaries. Choosing to respond to God sets us on a path of faith, where we can become active participants in the full realization of God's kin-dom, already here and not yet.

---

1   Frederick Buechner, *Wishful Thinking: A Seeker's ABC* (San Francisco: Harper San Francisco, 1993), 398.

2   The phrase, "kin-dom of God," was first coined by Ada Maria Isasi-Diaz. It emphasizes relationality, community, and equity as the basis of God's reign. It is an obvious contrast to systems of oppression and relations of domination.

CHAPTER 1

The Sacraments:
God's Claim on Our Lives

By George McClain and Tilda Norberg

TILDA'S STORY: DOING WHAT COMES NATURALLY

Distracted and hurried, I dashed into a huge IKEA furniture store one afternoon, intent on buying a set of sheets and just getting out of there. The aisles were crowded. Babies were fussing in their strollers. Shoppers were speaking, some loudly, in many languages.

Suddenly, above all the hubbub, a child's voice emerged: "Holy, holy, holy, Lord God of Hosts, heaven and earth are full of your glory. . . ."

I spun around and saw a boy, perhaps seven, with a girl who I guessed to be no older than four, sitting on a couch. The boy spoke slowly and reverently; the girl listened intently. Oblivious to the crowds, they were wrapped in a cocoon of rapt attention and, yes, worship. No one else seemed to notice the children, nor did I see a parent nearby. The boy continued to recite the entire Communion liturgy as the girl offered some of the liturgical responses. Together, they pretended to share bread and wine.

I was slowed down, drawn in, and greatly moved. Surely they did not really understand what they were doing, but they were responding instinctively to the sacredness and power of the ceremony and the presence of the Holy Spirit. I was struck with the realization that these two tiny humans were doing what is natural to all of us, responding to meaning that is beyond words, and they were doing it through the most treasured liturgy of the Christian church

THE POWER OF RITUAL

Something in us hungers mightily to express itself in ritual. It exists in every human culture, and it is part of what separates us from the rest of the animal kingdom. Only humans create rituals to express, for example, group identity and roles, community, passages to a new life stage, and most importantly, religious meaning.

For eons, human beings have used the language of ritual to express what is inexpressible through mere words. We form rituals out of art, music, symbolic objects, and physical actions, as well as carefully chosen text, to communicate our deepest longings and to relate to what is infinitely greater than us.

Rituals, no matter the context, are usually communal. Sharing a religious ritual with others gives authority and substance to these profound longings. A wedding, for instance, in which the couple makes vows in the presence of God, respected witnesses, and the people they love, holds much greater power and meaning than if one night over dinner the couple simply promises to stick together.

Through rituals, we are ushered from one stage of life to another, and these changes are recognized and celebrated communally. For example, when a girl turns fifteen in the Hispanic community, she often is given a *Quince Años,* or *Quinceañera,* celebration to formally recognize her passage to womanhood. The event usually begins with a church service, and some customs require the girl to dress in childish shoes. Our young friend, Margarita Ordoñez, wore bunny slippers to her *Quince Años* day. Later, she was solemnly presented with her first pair of high heels and a sophisticated woman's necklace. During the service, Ordoñez publicly thanked her parents for raising her and vowed to dedicate her new adult life to

God. Speeches by family and friends challenged her to remain faithful to the promises she had just made and welcomed her to adulthood. Before we went downstairs for a delicious Salvadoran meal, the gathered congregation promised to pray for her continued growth and maturity. This special celebration was a crucial milestone that Ordoñez will remember all her life.

Obviously, not all rituals are constructive. The human impulse to create rituals can be distorted to destroy rather than to build up, ridicule rather than encourage, exclude rather than embrace, or glorify violence instead of tolerance. Life-sapping rituals can be so destructive that the very word "ritual" is frightening for some survivors. For this reason, the words "liturgy" and "service" will be used to describe the Christian practices in this book.

In their most soul-nourishing form, rituals bind us to a principled community and affirm God's claim on our lives. Rituals can begin to shape how we feel about ourselves. Christian liturgies can provide an opening for the gospel to take deeper root in us. We receive the message again and again that:

- God loves us passionately as God's children;
- God wants to heal us in some way;
- God gives us somewhere to turn when life falls apart;
- God ensures that we are never alone;
- God views even the humblest life as a gift to be cherished;
- God is in charge of the world;
- Christ is able to transform our suffering, no matter how terrible it is; and
- God has given each of us something special to offer others.

Liturgies can help provide a way for us to declare what we know to be the truth, even if the truth is at odds with how we feel. They can help us separate our faith from our emotions; just because we may feel at the moment that God is not there, it does not mean that we have lost our faith.

Liturgies can also help us integrate our faith with our emotions, because we learn that God is with us in our emotional reactions, no matter how unpleasant. When a loved one dies, for example, we may become angry with God, be unable to pray, and feel spiritually dead inside. A funeral liturgy that declares the promise of eternal life can be a great comfort, taking us to an emotional place that we may be unable to get to by ourselves. The result can be a grounded, integrated faith that, even in times of greatest despair, God is still with us.

Liturgies can move us in remarkable ways. Most remarkable, though, is simply that God is in the midst of it all, penetrating our lives through our own innate capacity for creating ritual.

LOST AND FOUND: LITURGIES OF LIBERATION

In recent decades there's been a concern in The United Methodist Church about the loss of vitality in the practice of our two Christian sacraments, baptism and Holy Communion. The denomination has sponsored and ratified official studies of each sacrament, which are published in *The Book of Resolutions of The United Methodist Church,* as well as in helpful study editions with commentary by Gayle Felton, a major architect of both studies.[1] **A chief concern has to do with the apparent loss of the sense that not only are we engaging in sacred actions and speaking sacred words, but also that God is present and active in a special way.** The Methodist movement had its origin in the genius of Anglican priest John Wesley, who fashioned a "creative synthesis of sacramentalism and evangelism."[2] His gift was to join the sacramental understanding—that God actually offers grace and power through the sacraments—with an evangelical spirit that insists the individual must make a decision to embrace the grace and freedom God offers in the sacraments. The first emphasizes what God does; the second emphasizes our response. Wesley believed that both are necessary.

The loss of Wesley's creative synthesis has its roots in the historical development of American Methodism. With a scarcity of ordained leaders in the early church, access to the sacraments was limited, and "the sacramental teachings of Wesley tended to be ignored."[3] Scientific advances also slowly devalued the sacraments. A sense of mystery was replaced with a new focus on what was measurable and observable. Our capacity for reason began to overshadow our openness to divine revelation, and even to a sense of God's presence.

Alongside this, the decline of the sacraments also caused us to forget the essential conflict in human life between the kin-dom of God and "kingdoms" of this world. The doctrine of original sin—or, perhaps more accurately, all-pervasive sin—maintains that human beings, while made in the image of God, are born into a complicated, contradictory, and broken world. Sooner or later in our lives, we will encounter tragedy, disappointment, temptations, injustice, and violence. We will know the eroding effect of power, institutions, and customs gone awry.

But the sacraments are intended to remind us that God will not desert any of us, ever. God's creation of us isn't over when we are born; it continues throughout our lives. God is there, constantly redeeming and healing and turning things upside down. God even continues to be in sweaty labor to birth the world, panting and pushing to make all things new.

In Wesley's original vision, God's power to confront human brokenness is both revealed and affirmed in the sacraments. Communion and baptism are assurances of God's desire to be in relationship with us. They are conduits through which God works to protect, heal, transform, and liberate us. They echo Paul's declaration that nothing can "separate us from the love of God in Christ Jesus": "neither death, nor life, nor angels, nor rulers, nor things present, nor things to come, nor powers, nor height, nor depth, nor anything in all creation" (Romans 8:39, 38).

Which brings us back to mystery.

Christian experience teaches us that God chooses to be especially self-revealing in the sacraments. Why is this so? While mystery itself suggests we can't expect to have clear answers, surely the sacraments reflect God's desire to be close to us. The sacraments are not magic, but we can learn to expect something extraordinary from them. At best, we can open our hearts to what God might do. We can ask what God is communicating in this sacrament on this day. We can actively recall that God's presence permeates all things. We can let the sacrament remind us that any moment, any situation, any time can be a venue for God to surprise us.

Our hope is that this exploration of the sacraments will open us to new ways of sacramental living, give us new hearts to follow Christ as agents of the reign of God, and give us new eyes to see the power of God revealed everywhere in our lives.

THE COVENANT OF BAPTISM

The sacrament of baptism is often practiced casually in our churches. Infant baptism may be undertaken simply as a family custom. Teenagers or adults may request baptism just because it is a requirement for church membership, a "hoop to jump through." They may undergo little or no preparation.

Think about it: Do you believe there is a spiritual urgency about baptism? Does God claim you in a unique way through baptism? We believe the answer to both questions is yes.

Compare your own experience and belief with Larry's baptism experience.

LARRY'S STORY: BAPTISM DENIED

For most of his life, Larry knew what it was like to feel worthless and ignored.

Discarded by his parents, left as a child to survive on the streets, imprisoned at a young age for being in the wrong place at the wrong time, Larry had spent more time in prison than out.

Providentially, God's grace was evident when some trustworthy inmates took him under their wings and taught him to read, thus whetting his appetite for learning. Remarkably, he eventually earned a bachelor's degree and even a master's degree in theology. He became a source of counsel and wisdom for many struggling inmates.

Through it all, Larry heard God calling and claiming him. He was asked by others—and by God, he'd say—to help run a theological studies program for other inmates, a sort of mini-seminary. Together with outside clergy, he assisted with the teaching.

By now, Larry was feeling God's invitation to cement his new identity as a child of God. Enough talking about faith, he felt. Time to seal the covenant with God. He knew that meant to be baptized. So he approached the prison chaplain, who agreed to baptize Larry soon.

But, that "soon" never came. The chaplain, for whatever personal reasons, kept postponing the baptism. Larry's heart was broken. Each time, he prepared himself, spending special days in a personal retreat; then a day or so before, the chaplain invariably postponed the event. Larry had never belonged to a family, and the church had filled that void. He wanted to mark what God was doing in his life in the way that Christians throughout the centuries had marked their entrance into the community of faith. He simply wanted to be baptized! And the more it was delayed, the more he yearned for the sacred water and words. Never was it clearer that the sacrament of baptism could be so crucial to someone's identity.

Word of Larry's predicament reached the volunteer theological teachers he worked with. Mostly clergy, they were incensed that the chaplain had not baptized someone so well prepared and with such great desire. They wanted to step in, but they knew they were allowed in the prison as educators, not clergy. They didn't want to usurp the chaplain's role and run afoul of any prison rules.

Finally, one had the bold idea to baptize Larry as an "educational exercise" in a class on liturgies. It would be a classroom demonstration, but it would also be an actual baptism. The men in the class wondered, would this hark back to the baptisms that secretly took place in the Roman catacombs? And so Larry experienced, under these strange circumstances, what he called the best day of his life: "I was baptized!"

For those of us who know Larry, this was a profound reminder of the meaning of baptism. His deep need caused others to think more seriously about their own baptism. Larry reminded us that in our baptism we know who we are, not only as children of God but also as those who take sides against the influences and forces working against God's kin-dom.

A BOLD APPROACH

At its heart, baptism is a bold act. We are marked with God's stamp that echoes the very story of creation: "God saw everything that he had made, and indeed, it was very good" (Genesis 1:31). God says a resounding yes to us in our baptism. Yes, I claim you as my own. Whatever happens to you, I will be there with you, seeking to redeem you, bringing you to your right mind, holding you in my arms, rejoicing in your beauty and uniqueness.

This promise is movingly stated in the hymn, "I Was There to Hear Your Borning Cry," by John Ylvisaker:

> I was there to hear your borning cry, I'll be there when you are old.
> I rejoiced the day you were baptized, to see your life unfold.
>
> I was there when you were but a child, with a faith to suit you well;
> In a blaze of light you wandered off to find where demons dwell.
>
> When you heard the wonder of the Word I was there to cheer
> you on;
> You we raised to praise the living Lord, to whom you now belong.[4]

In this situation of both struggle for our very selves and continued growth and healing, the covenant of baptism is a crucial channel of what we call the grace of God.

Truly, God is all about grace.

"Grace pervades our understanding of Christian faith and life," according to United Methodist teaching. "By grace we mean the unde-served, unmerited, and loving action of God in human existence through the ever-present Holy Spirit."[5]

The lyrics of one of our best-loved hymns, "Amazing Grace," also help illustrate the dimensions of grace as United Methodists understand them.

Prevenient (or preparing) grace is the grace that "comes before" any re-sponse of ours. This grace of God has been there for us from the beginning, silently at work to bring us to the point of awareness of our shortcomings and of the insubstantial "gods" in our lives. It offers God's invitation to turn our lives over to God. Hymn writer John Newton powerfully describes his own transformation from captain of a slave ship to ardent abolitionist:

> Amazing grace! How sweet the sound that saved a wretch like me!
> I once was lost, but now am found; was blind, but now I see.

> 'Twas grace that taught my heart to fear, and grace my fears relieved; how precious did that grace appear the hour I first believed.[6]

It was God's prevenient grace, or grace of preparation, that taught New-ton's heart "to fear," that is, to tremble in awareness of how his life was such a denial of the person God had intended him to be. Then, it was God's *justify-ing (or forgiving) grace* that restored him to his true self and reconciled him to God. This "precious" grace enabled him to know himself immediately as a freed and forgiven sinner.

Wesley described prevenient grace as the "porch of religion" and justify-ing grace as the "door of religion." The actual "house of religion" is the realm of *sanctifying (or perfecting) grace.*[7] This is the life of faith in which one grows, with the aim to be totally filled, or perfected, with the love of Christ. In this grace we are sustained in life, empowered with the gifts of God, equipped as disciples, and led ever more intimately to our true home in God.

> Through many dangers, toils, and snares, I have already come;
> 'tis grace hath brought me safe thus far, and grace will lead me

home. The Lord has promised good to me, his word my hope se-
cures; he will my shield and portion be, as long as life endures.[8]

This description of the three kinds of grace, especially prevenient grace, helps answer the often-asked question: what difference does it make if we were baptized in infancy, totally unaware of what was happening?

Infant baptism activates the promise of God for that child. The parents and/or sponsors, as well as the congregation, promise to raise the child with the faith that God will be at work through them. At some point, we will become aware of our infant baptism, which has the potential to provide direction to our lives. Customarily, when we approach our teenage years, we are offered instruction and the opportunity to claim our baptismal vows for ourselves and to join the church as confessing members through the rite of confirmation.

The process of growth in grace, Wesley emphasized, is a synergy between the human and the divine. God initiates but waits for our response. To welcome God's work into our lives, we must give awareness, attention, and consent to the things of God.

For a deeper, or "heart," response to Christian baptism, take a look with us at the "Congregational Reaffirmation of the Baptismal Covenant,"[9] which has become increasingly popular in United Methodist churches. In it, we reaffirm the life-defining vows made for us or by us at our baptism.

The baptismal service, whether for infants or adults, begins with gratitude for the continuing biblical drama of God's giving, restoring, and liberating. We praise God's creative powers, recalling the first words of the Bible that, "In the beginning when God created the heavens and the earth, the earth was a formless void. . . ." (Genesis 1:1–2).

> When nothing existed but chaos,
> you swept across the dark waters
> and brought forth light.[10]

We praise God's saving and liberating mercy in human events, particularly through water. We lift up the experiences of the Hebrew people that have inspired people of faith across the generations: liberation from slavery and domination (Exodus 1–15) and deliverance to a new land of promise (the book of Joshua).

> When you saw your people as slaves in Egypt,
> you led them to freedom through the sea.
> Their children you brought through the Jordan
> to the land which you promised.[11]

The liturgy then moves on to the great events of the New Covenant: Jesus' coming as Emmanuel, "God with us"; his baptism by John; and his anointing by the Spirit (Matthew 3:13–17). We commemorate Jesus' calling of his disciples (Luke 5:1–11, 27–32) and, by extension, his calling of all those baptized to be his disciples:

> In the fullness of time you sent Jesus,
> nurtured in the water of a womb.
> He was baptized by John and anointed by your Spirit.
> He called his disciples
> to share in the baptism of his death and resurrection
> and to make disciples of all nations.[12]

Finally, we celebrate the washing away of sin and our dying and rising with Christ, and we pray again for the gift of the Holy Spirit upon us through the water:

> Pour out your Holy Spirit,
> and by this gift of water call to our remembrance
> the grace declared to us in our baptism.
> For you have washed away our sins,
> and you clothe us with righteousness throughout our lives,
> that dying and rising with Christ
> we may share in his final victory.[13]

Of course, it's easy to simply go through a service without really participating. We've probably all done it—reciting or listening without thinking about the words, or perhaps even making a mental list of groceries to pick up on the way home.

But taken to heart, these are living words. If we allow them to touch us, we can know ourselves as part of God's plan for a new humanity and a new creation. We are forcefully reminded that even we—with our seemingly ordinary lives in one small corner of creation—are incorporated into the grand design of the creator and savior God. We are not simply bystanders. God calls to us through the baptismal questions and points to our part in the divine plan revealed in Jesus Christ and witnessed in scripture:

> Do you renounce the spiritual forces of wickedness,
>   reject the evil powers of this world,
>   and repent of your sin?[14]

Renounce. Reject. Repent. These are strong, vigorous actions God calls us to take. They remind us of the boldness we need to employ. As Christians, we acknowledge sin as a fact of life. We are born into a world in which God's good creation has been twisted and distorted by human customs, power structures, institutions, and values that are not of God. In the New Testament, they are called principalities, rulers, and powers.

Some scholars explain that, in New Testament times, these three entities were thought to be part of God's original good creation. After all, some form of government is needed.[15] Public safety must be provided for; economic systems are necessary to produce and distribute vital commodities; institutions can bring us together to serve the common good and care for the young, the sick, and the homeless. People of God organize into congregations and denominations with ordained and lay leaders. But along the way, these structures may become derailed. If they do, they can take away human dignity, institutionalize greed and lust for power, and wed us to unjust ways of organizing society, allowing some to suffer with too little while giving others too much. They can lure us into an apathy that accepts the outrageous as simply "the way things are."

Make no mistake: as Christians, we are called to side with God's reign and to oppose the "spiritual forces of wickedness." But renouncing, rejecting, and repenting are only the beginning. Conversion must show itself in action. And so we are asked:

> Do you accept the freedom and power God gives you
> to resist evil, injustice, and oppression
> in whatever forms they present themselves?[16]

We are graced by God with the gift of making decisions. We are called to join in God's mission to resist what is not of God. How often we resign ourselves to injustice, thinking we are powerless! Our baptismal vows do not allow us to wallow in self-pity or our own perceived weakness, to give up in the face of what harms human life. Nor can we just give in to our own destructive patterns and compulsions. We don't stop seeking God's healing. We are never to reject the "freedom and power God gives you." Wesley called this the imperative of "holy living." In other words, we are called to walk justly! And in doing so, we place ourselves in the force field of God's "amazing grace."

> Do you confess Jesus Christ as your Savior,
> put your whole trust in his grace,
> and promise to serve him as your Lord,
> in union with the church which Christ has opened
> to people of all ages, nations, and races?[17]

Our baptismal vow is to confess one savior and seek to reflect his light. We are to become besotted lovers of the world in all its messiness and pain. We are to allow God to love us even when we don't even love ourselves. We are to depend more and more on God to re-create us, again and again.

None of this is simple, but taking this vow does not imply perfection. We will continue to miss the mark, to choose the wrong way, to slide into whatever is easiest. But our baptismal promise is to start again—and again—with God's help.

> According to the grace given to you,
> will you remain faithful members of Christ's holy church
> and serve as Christ's representatives in the world?[18]

Not just clergy, deaconesses, and home missioners have what United Methodists call a "representative ministry." We all do. In whatever we do, however ordinary or extraordinary, we are representing Christ. Martin Luther even exhorted us to be "little Christs," followers who imitate Christ so thoroughly that others easily recognize Christ in us. What a daunting challenge! For this we need a continual infusion of God's "grace sufficient" (2 Corinthians 12:9). We find indispensable spiritual nourishment for this great journey in the other sacrament Jesus instituted.

HOLY COMMUNION

TILDA'S STORY: HUNGRY FOR THE EUCHARIST

Ever since I was a teenager I have loved the Eucharist. Growing up, I always wished my Methodist church offered it more often than four times a year. In college, I seldom missed the seven o'clock Wednesday morning Communion at Michigan State's Wesley Foundation. Later, I attended Union Seminary's weekly Eucharist, which was presented in a wide variety of worship traditions.

The more I participated, the hungrier I became for Holy Communion. After I was ordained, but not working in a local church, I led Communion services in a psychiatric hospital, in my office, and in people's homes. Sometimes, when friends and I would hike in the woods, I would carry a small Communion kit in my backpack because I knew that we would stop somewhere to rest and worship.

My most important Communion experience happened weekly in the East Harlem Protestant parish where I worked for all three of my seminary years. Very early each Sunday, I would take the bus to a posh address: Fifth Avenue and One Hundredth Street. I then walked along One Hundredth Street toward the East River, passing Madison, Park, Lexington, and Third Avenues, with each block becoming increasingly run-down.

By the time I crossed Second Avenue and was in the parish's neighborhood, the crowded tenements were not fit for anyone to live in. Loud music blared out of the many bodegas—even early on Sunday morning—and impatient drivers leaned on their horns. Squealing children played in the street amid garbage (which was not collected nearly as often as it was in more affluent neighborhoods). Addicts scratched themselves as they leaned against buildings. At the time, this block was one of the worst in the city.

The dilapidated storefront of The Church of the Resurrection was down several steps from the sidewalk, and the flimsy door was no barrier to the smells and sounds of the street. Our church had a low ceiling, dingy walls, and about twenty battered metal folding chairs in two concentric circles. But the altar was always artistically set with a snowy white cloth and a beautiful pottery chalice and plate. Faithful Christians gathered from the neighborhood. The carefully planned liturgy was rooted in the gospel response to the tragedy and promise of East Harlem. Street people drifted in and out, some high, some curious, some hungry. There were prayers for the sick and for justice, as well as announcements for Bible study and political demonstrations.

Weekly Eucharist was formative for me here. It said that God was present, maybe even *most present*, in despair and desperate need, in pain and poverty, in addiction and stench and constant noise. Here the saints gathered—people who knew joy and hope and spent their lives helping neighbors with their own meager resources. Here were shining faith, dignity, and beauty. Here there were no divisions between street people and seminary professors, the old and young, rich and poor, black and white, male and female. And here was God's presence brightly shining in bread and cup.

GEORGE'S STORY: CALLED TO A DEEPER PLACE

Like many Christians, I have not always centered my faith and practice on our two fundamental sacraments. I also must confess, with some embarrassment as someone ordained fifty years ago, that I have long felt uncomfortable, even afraid, when I preside at the Eucharist.

Like many United Methodists brought up in my generation, I have looked upon Holy Communion mostly as an occasion to repent of sin, to remember Jesus' sacrifice, or to deepen my experience of Christian community. But, I've also felt as if something might be happening there that I don't understand—and I don't like to do anything I don't understand.

When Tilda and I hosted a midweek Holy Communion in our home, I was happy to let Tilda or someone else lead the service. Truth be told, I avoided doing the consecration of the bread and cup.

But I must own up: I have recently been called to a deeper place. It began with studying the problems that Apostle Paul experienced with the earliest Christians in Corinth. Paul had invested a year and a half to establish this pioneering community of believers. He instructed these new Jesus followers to be a colony of God within the emperor's colony. They were to be God's alternative to the ways of greed, social climbing, status seeking, and worship of rank and position.

But within a couple of years, Paul learned that this new commonwealth of God was being infected by the prevailing disease. They were dividing into factions, and some were living by the "wisdom of the world" instead of the "wisdom of God."

This disease, Paul learned, was even infecting the Lord's Supper. At that time, the sacred ceremony was genuinely a full meal, a kind of church potluck. Because of an ongoing famine, some of the poorer congregants counted on the common meal to stave off starvation. But the better nourished were getting to the house church earlier than the workers, peasants, and slaves and were eating up the food and drink. Some were even getting drunk (1 Corinthians 11:17–34).

In his letter, Paul angrily holds the haughty, selfish ones responsible that many "are weak and ill and some have died" (verse 30). He sternly reminds them that the table of the Lord is all about sharing. When Jesus said, "do this to remember me," he was not just speaking of eating and drinking, but of sharing the essentials of life with the less fortunate. The Lord's Supper is a challenge to the unequal ways of the world. It is about how we share the blessings of life, at all the tables of life.

I heard another call to a deeper place as a result of studying United Methodism's understanding of the Eucharist. Like the study of baptism, it sought to regain the historic Wesleyan balance between the sacramental and the evangelical. Officially adopted in 2004, it stresses that Holy Communion is not just a memory of deeds, teachings, and sacrifice.[19] We, as a church, assert with a new clarity that the Eucharistic act of sharing the basic elements of food and drink embodies the living presence of the risen Christ among us.

Reflecting on this declaration, I decided that at my next Holy Communion I would be as open as I could to these emerging perspectives: Christ is really present and Jesus' command "Do this," includes the radical sharing of all of God's gifts, material as well as spiritual.

So here I am, at The Church in the Village (United Methodist) in New York City, with a class for prospective deaconesses and home missioners. As I settle comfortably into my pew, the presiding pastor slips over and asks whether I would join other ordained elders at the appropriate time to consecrate the elements. What could I say, but of course. My part of the text, she said, would be marked clearly at the Communion table.

After a stirring sermon and a moving solo from Handel's "The Messiah" about preparing the way of the Lord, I go forward to join the other clergy at the table. I look to see my part, and it is the very heart of the Eucharist, the consecrating words of Jesus: "Take, eat; this is my body, which is given for you. . . . This is my blood of the new covenant."

"Oh my God," I say to myself—half irreverent exclamation, half prayer.

In a moment, it's my turn to speak, but the words seem to stick in my throat. I can feel tears swell. Something's happening, I realize. I'm invoking the real presence of Christ. And yes, Christ is really here, now, in and through and beyond these shared elements. I make it through the words of consecration, hoping it's not obvious that my voice is breaking. Thankfully, it's someone else's turn now.

In a flash, it seems, I'm being offered "the body of Christ." I suddenly notice who's giving this to me: a New Testament professor I last saw in my prison work. I had been teaching New Testament there; she had spent an evening in a training event for prospective theology teachers in prison. The state had just closed the prison; I could never return to this place where I had been ministered to by God's poor, as perhaps nowhere else in my life. As I take the bread, time and space are transformed: I am back in the prison with her, with the men I had grown to love.

Then my mind and heart go every which way at once. I am back with the early Corinthian believers struggling to be generous in a selfish world, to love in a loveless place. I am with Jesus at the Last Supper, that Passover meal replete with both human desperation and hope in God's liberation. I am with the risen Christ in all the struggles for justice. I am even at the Final Banquet when Christ and his ways will be all in all. And I am right there, around this table, in this city, on this day, receiving these traditional gifts in a radically new way. I am stunned.

I sit back down in the pew and sob. The hymn comes to mind: "He touched me. Something happened, and now I know, he touched me and made me whole."[20] The presence of Christ: yes, it's real!

A RICH BANQUET

At its most profound, Holy Communion, or the Eucharist, offers a rich banquet of meaning, memory, and expectation. Rooted in the sharing of an ordinary meal, it makes the extraordinary claim that Christ is present and all creation is holy. Instituted on the eve of Christ's trial and death, it joyfully celebrates the living Christ among us. Though shamed by historical divisions, squabbles, and exclusiveness, the Eucharist still proclaims the underlying unity of all Christians.

Sometimes celebrated in secrecy amid political oppression, cruelty, and injustice, Holy Communion shines with the radical message of justice and dignity for all people. All are welcome here; all are fed. Around this table, the kin-dom has already come and God's will is being done on earth as it is in heaven.

Each time we come to the table, we can expect the grace of God to be manifested in a variety of ways. We can be confident that God will shape our attention and awareness to meet us where we are. Our job, then, is to be as open as possible and pay attention to God's movement in us.

The following are some ways you may experience a foretaste of God's reign when you gather around the Lord's Table:

You may know the Holy Spirit is active. Each time you go to Holy Communion, trust as best you can that God will "pour out" the Holy Spirit on "us gathered here, and on these gifts of bread and wine."[21] Pray with confidence that through the same Holy Spirit "we may be for the world the body of Christ."[22] That's a tall order, but God's promises are trustworthy. If your faith weakens, turn this mystery over to God, as you turn your life to God. Ask God to nurture your faith. Open yourself to the realm of mystery where everything is not explained by science and reason. Hold your "why" questions loosely, but with expectation, and wait. Answers to those questions may catch you by surprise.

You may experience the presence of Christ. The New Testament writers and the church throughout the ages have sought appropriate metaphors to describe a mystical oneness with Christ. Paul's writing frequently uses the image of being "in Christ."[23] Another image to hold is of Jesus himself breaking bread with you. Jody Halstead, a United Methodist laywoman from Asheville, North Carolina, puts it this way: "When I take Holy Communion, I feel as though I'm filling myself with Christ."

You may grow and be healed. God is constantly pouring out love to nurture you. Often it is during the Eucharist that this tender love is poured out in special measure. Be open to glimmers of any healing invitation you might receive from God. Remember, "Much of this healing is spiritual, but it also includes the healing of our thoughts and emotions, of our minds and bodies, of our attitudes and relationships."[24] Through God's grace you may be healed in the Eucharist. Then, in the lovely phrase of Henri Nouwen, you may become a "wounded healer,"[25] equipped to allow the love of Christ to splash out of you and into situations of suffering and need.

You may be stirred to offer thanks. In the Communion liturgy, we say, "It is right, and a good and joyful thing, always and everywhere to give thanks to you . . . "[26] More and more, we are referring to Holy Communion as the *Eucharist*, a Greek-derived word meaning "thanksgiving." Give thanks for your blessings and for the ways God is redeeming your mistakes, wrong turns, and tragedies. Give thanks for God's power to free you from bondage and create signs of the new creation.

You may be motivated to work for reconciliation. Holy Communion is a symbol of our unity in Christ, even as this is not yet realized. Turning again to those early Corinthian believers, we recall Paul was deeply concerned that those who were to model a new kind of community were themselves torn apart. He reminded them that they were "baptized into one body" and at the Lord's Supper they were all to "partake of one bread." In the sharing of the "one loaf," they were "sharing in the body of Christ" (1 Corinthians 10:16–17, 12:12–14).

To celebrate the Lord's Supper means to lay aside differences and embody the new creation and its wholeness. In Holy Communion, Christ calls you to work for reconciliation in your church, in your United Methodist family, and in the whole Christian family, that we "may all be one" (John 17:21). This is challenging, given our sometimes deep divisions, even over the Eucharist itself. If you find yourself judging others' customs and beliefs regarding the Lord's Supper, try confessing your judgment and asking that Christ heal you.

Years ago we visited the ecumenical religious order at Taizé, France, and happened upon a youth conference for both Protestants and

Catholics. Though the two groups took Communion in separate services, what we've never forgotten was how all the participants joined together in the courtyard to share bread and grapes as a living sign of both the scandal of our divided churches and our belief that, in the most profound way, we are already united in Christ.

You may feel compelled to work for inclusion. All are welcome at the Lord's Table, and all God's children sit in the presence of Jesus—even those who do not use Jesus' name. There is no room at the Eucharistic table for distinctions of rich and poor, white and black, old and young, educated and illiterate, gay and straight. As you come to this sacred table, you are in solidarity with a suffering, broken, and striving humanity. No exceptions.

You may want to act for justice and liberation. For disciples of Jesus, the Lord's Table becomes a model for the whole human community. None should be weak or die of hunger. All the gifts of God are to be shared with all the people of God.

When you participate in Holy Communion, reaffirm to yourself that love and justice are the way and will of God. Even if it is painful, open your eyes to the ways of the world that benefit some people and leave so many on the margins. Remember, too, the systemic destruction of the natural world that is occurring. Ask God to make clear what your part in loving the world is. Let the rest go, trusting that God still has, in the words of the traditional American spiritual, "the whole world in his hands."

You may experience a feeling of hope. Next time you participate in Holy Communion, take a big glorious taste and swig at the heavenly banquet, celebrating God's victory over sin, shame, evil, and death. Allow this hope to feed you in the most difficult times. Live on tiptoe, looking for God to be revealed in all dimensions of life. Let yourself be nourished by sacramental grace. Keep striving to be formed in the image of Christ and to be made an instrument for the transformation of the world. [27]

STICKING WITH THE EUCHARIST DURING DRY TIMES

Even after all we've said, you may still experience Holy Communion as a dry recital of abstract words or formulas. Perhaps it's still something you're just enduring, annoyed by how much longer than usual the Sunday service will be. Or maybe you mostly find it boring, less a celebration and a thanksgiving than a monotonous ceremony with stiff, creaky words.

If you are in a spiritual desert right now, be assured that this is a common experience. Hang on, and keep participating in the Eucharist. Remind yourself that God is at work even if you don't perceive it. Simple participation, even in a rote manner, can plant seeds in your soul that may germinate later. Words and phrases like "grace," "sin," "hope," "forgiveness," "love of God," or "eternal life" may blaze forth to touch something deep within you. Liturgical actions like breaking bread, drinking from a sacred cup, or kneeling in reverence may suddenly resonate with special meaning in the midst of life.[28]

Here are some other suggestions for those experiencing a dry time:

- Prepare yourself by noticing what is going on in the deepest recesses of your heart. What deliverance are you yearning for? Write it down, if you are drawn to journaling.

- Pray for healing before the Communion service. Summon whatever faith you have that Christ will indeed fill you with goodness and grant you freedom. In particular, ask Jesus to touch your deepest hurts, most profound doubts, and shakiest beliefs. Keep asking, and trust as best you can that this will be so.

- Notice what happens within you as you participate in the liturgy, sing the hymns, hear the scriptures, recite your prayers, and make your offering. Try not to discount any awareness before you have time to sit with it.

- Give thanks to God for the divine grace working within you and in the world, even if you don't experience it at the moment.

LOVE FEAST: A RITUAL OF THE HEART

The Love Feast is a service that was common in the early days of Methodism and, from its beginnings, was often led by women. While distinct from Holy Communion, it offers some of the blessings of the sacrament.

The Love Feast can be led by anyone, so it is appropriate when no one present is authorized to administer the sacrament. It emphasizes the boundless love of God and finds its uniqueness in focusing on heart-to-heart sharing of how God is at work in our lives. The service, while orderly, offers more spontaneity and less formality than Holy Communion. It can be held any place suitable for a religious gathering, including a home.

The service typically includes hymns, prayers, scripture, sharing of bread or some other baked good, collection for the poor, sharing of drink, and testimonies. Historical background, instructions, and a suggested order of service can be found in *The United Methodist Book of Worship*.[29]

HOW TO LIVE YOUR BAPTISM

- Promote the use of the "Congregational Reaffirmation of the Baptismal Covenant," found in *The United Methodist Hymnal* in your church.

- Meditate on your baptismal vows in the moments before Sunday worship begins, or take a day or more in retreat to reflect on the gifts and call of your baptism.

- Reflect on the "spiritual forces of wickedness," "the evil powers of the world," and "sin" as you see them in your community, in the world, in yourself. Pray to know what it means in your life to "accept the freedom and power God gives you to resist evil, injustice, and oppression."

- Ask how God wants to heal or change you. Be open to images, intuitions, impressions, and memories that seem to be God's answer.

- Pray for God's healing when you find yourself in despair or tempted. Try declaring, "I am baptized!" Add your own affirmations. Ask God to teach you how much you are loved.

- Pray to see yourself as one who is stamped "good" in spite of any shame or self-hatred you may carry. Pray that God will show you how to claim your own goodness.

---

1   Gayle Carlton Felton, *By Water and the Spirit* (Nashville: Discipleship Resources, 1996) and *This Holy Mystery* (Nashville: Discipleship Resources, 2004).

2   "By Water and the Spirit," Resolution 8013, *The Book of Resolutions of the United Methodist Church, 2008* (Nashville: Abingdon Press, 2008,) 944.

3   "By Water and the Spirit," Resolution 8013, *The Book of Resolutions*, 942.

4   "I Was There to Hear Your Borning Cry," *The Faith We Sing* (Nashville: Abingdon Press, 2000), 2051.

5   *The Book of Discipline of The United Methodist Church, 2008* (Nashville: The United Methodist Publishing House, 2008), ¶45.

6 "Amazing Grace," *The United Methodist Hymnal* (Nashville, Abingdon Press, 1993), 378; Carlton Young, *Companion to the United Methodist Hymnal* (Nashville: Abingdon Press, 1993), 206-207, 84-85.

7 Charles Yrigoyen, Jr., *John Wesley: Holiness of Heart and Life* (Nashville: Abingdon Press, 1996), 36.

8 Ibid., 387.

9 "Congregational Reaffirmation of the Baptismal Covenant," *The United Methodist Hymnal,* 50–53.

10 Ibid., 51.

11 Ibid., 51.

12 Ibid., 52.

13 Ibid., 52.

14 Ibid., 50.

15 See, for instance, Walter Wink, *The Powers That Be: Theology for a New Millennium* (New York: Doubleday, 1998) and *Engaging the Powers: Discernment and Resistance in a World of Domination* (Minneapolis: Fortress Press, 1992).

16 "Congregational Reaffirmation of the Baptismal Covenant," *The United Methodist Hymnal,* 50.

17 Ibid.

18 Ibid.

19 Gayle Carlton Felton, *This Holy Mystery: A United Methodist Understanding of Holy Communion* (Nashville: Discipleship Resources, 2005). Includes the basic United Methodist document, plus commentary and study guide by Felton.

20 "He Touched Me," *The United Methodist Hymnal,* 367.

21 "A Service of Word and Table I," *The United Methodist Hymnal,* 6.

22 Ibid.

23 For instance: "So if anyone is in Christ, there is a new creation. . . ." 2 Corinthians 5:17.

24 "This Holy Mystery: A United Methodist Understanding of Holy Communion," Resolution 8014, *The Book of Resolutions,* 972.

25 Henri J. M. Nouwen, *The Wounded Healer: Ministry in Contemporary Society* (New York: Doubleday, 1972).

26 "A Service of Word and Table I," *The United Methodist Hymnal,* 9.

27 "This Holy Mystery," Resolution 8014, *The Book of Resolutions,* 971.

28 Tom F. Driver, *The Magic of Ritual: Our Need for Liberating Rites that Transform our Lives and Our Communities* (New York: HarperCollins Publishers/Harper San Francisco, 1991), 196.

29 *The United Methodist Book of Worship* (Nashville: The United Methodist Publishing House, 1992), 581–584.

CHAPTER 2

Keeping the Sacramental Vision

By George McClain and Tilda Norberg

I n the last chapter, we learned that the sacraments are radical events that invite Christians to see our lives differently. When we gather around the table or font, timeworn habits, roles, and attitudes are turned upside down. We are called to attention and asked to open up, give up, take in, and dive in.

In the sacraments, God addresses us personally. Christ is present, as near as breath, and at work in each person. We are asked to see every moment of our lives as a venue for God's power and healing.

But here is the part many of us might slide over: in the sacraments, we are also beckoned to embrace God's vision of justice, mercy, and peace for all people.

The personal and the political: are you able to heed both of these dimensions? To illustrate their interconnection, we are going to take a fresh look at two familiar Gospel stories. The first is Jesus' gutsy triumphal entry into Jerusalem; the second is Jesus' delicious conversation with his old friends Mary and Martha. As you engage in these stories, ask yourself: How are you challenged? Intrigued? Put off? Do you see these stories, and perhaps your own life, in a new way? How do they give you additional insight into living sacramentally? Pay attention to your reactions.

TWO PROCESSIONS

There were two processions into Jerusalem that fateful Passover week, though one has long been forgotten. In New Testament times, however, everyone knew about the Roman occupation forces marching into the Holy City at the beginning of Passover week.[1] Coming from their seaside garrison of Caesarea—named after Emperor Caesar Augustus—the Roman procession was led by majestic horses and chariots and followed by legionnaires bristling with arms. Imagine how the populace must have cringed at the clanking of armor, the glint of steel, the din of drums and fanfare.

Pontius Pilate, ruling in the name of Emperor Tiberius, entered the Jews' holy city in force to send an unmistakable message to any potential "messiahs," troublemakers, or thieves: do not, under any circumstances, use the Jews' historical memory of liberation from slavery to stir up the huge Passover crowds![2] He had reason to be wary: the Jews had always been difficult for outsiders to rule; furthermore, the parallels between the harsh and cruel life of slavery under the Pharaoh and Roman occupation were obvious.

Virtually unnoticed at the time was the other procession, the one the Gospel writers tell us about. Among the few nonviolent forms of resistance available to oppressed people is mockery, and this procession cleverly mocked the arrogance of imperial Roman rule. In this risky alternative procession, the itinerant preacher Jesus was cheered on by his followers from the remote region of Galilee. He processed into Jerusalem, not on a magnificent, decorated steed, but on a humble, borrowed donkey. The symbolism of the donkey underscored the message of resistance. Centuries before, the Hebrew prophet Zechariah had written that their king would enter Jerusalem "triumphant and victorious, . . . humble and riding on a donkey . . . and he shall command peace to the nations . . ." (Zechariah 9:9–10).

Pilate's procession from the west embodied the power, wealth, oppression, and violence of the empire that ruled most of the known world. Jesus' procession from the east embodied an alternative vision, the kindom of God, built on peace and justice.[3]

The one riding on the lowly beast had been attracting crowds and attention in Galilee as he decried the defiling of the Israelites' ancient covenant with their liberating God. Jesus announced his ministry "to bring good news to the poor . . . to let the oppressed go free . . . ." (Luke 4:18). In his travels, Jesus healed the sick, fed the poor, and taught his followers about a kin-dom of God that upended the ways of the ruling empire: "Blessed are you who are poor, for yours is the kingdom of God . . . . But woe to you who are rich, for you have received your consolation" (Luke 6:20, 24). "Blessed are the peacemakers, for they will be called children of God" (Matthew 5:9). Now, the one teaching these provocations was leading his ragtag followers into the very heart of a domination system anchored in the collusion between religious leaders and colonial officials. And Jesus' followers, rejecting the divine claims of imperial power, hailed him as the one who "comes in the name [that is, power] of the Lord" (Mark 11:9). A serious confrontation was in the making.

You know the rest of the Holy Week story. Jesus upset the authorities with his teachings. He sealed his fate when he stormed into the sacred precincts of the temple, driving out the extortionist moneychangers, charging that the temple authorities were a "den of robbers." He symbolically reclaimed the temple for the poor and marginalized, as a "house of prayer for all the nations" (Mark 11:17). By then the Roman authorities, egged on by their temple collaborators, had had enough, and taking no chances, they sent a message to his followers by executing him by crucifixion, the ultimate disgrace.

This whole dramatic week puts Jesus' real presence, religious and political, on public display. His entrance into the precincts of public power was God's gift to humanity and Jesus' model of sacramental living. In the private gathering with his closest followers for a "last supper," he underscored his total offering of himself for them and for all: "Take, eat; this is my body which is given for you. Do this in remembrance of me."[4]

Jesus charged the disciples to remember the week, including how he:

■ mocked Roman imperial pretensions;

- proclaimed the God of Israel, not Caesar, as Lord;
- exposed the corruption and collusion of the religious leadership;
- attacked elitism and arrogance;
- suffered death for the sake of God's kin-dom; and
- showed that beyond death is resurrection and vindication in God.

Throughout Holy Week, Jesus gave himself so we might carry on God's work, or as the Communion liturgy puts it, so we "might be for the world the body of Christ."[5]

Sacramental living is not for the faint of heart: It is to challenge the cruel, ruthless, callous, exploitative ways of the world. It is to be vulnerable to suffering for the sake of righteousness. Finally, it is to join in the vindication of God, for "blessed are those who are persecuted for righteousness's sake, for theirs is the kingdom of heaven" (Matthew 5:10). Taking the fullness of Christ within us—his body and blood—we, too, are empowered to be the real presence of Christ in the world.

AT HOME WITH MARY AND MARTHA

Reconciling the public firebrand Jesus with the gentle, personal Jesus can be a challenge. But it is a challenge that Christ demands of us. We are not serving a split-personality savior. Instead, both aspects of Jesus are integrated into a cohesive whole, as another episode from his ministry (Luke 10:38–42) illustrates.

Jesus' dear friends Martha and Mary have invited him to their home. As the scene opens, we find Mary sitting at Jesus' feet, implying that she was his disciple and student, a remarkable distinction for a woman of that time. Meanwhile, Martha was worried and distracted "by many tasks." She appeared irritated at Jesus, who seemed, as she put it, to "not care that my sister has left me to do all the work by myself." Calling tenderly to her, "Martha, Martha," and modeling the compassion he taught, Jesus lovingly pointed Martha toward what was most important, "the better part": to be his disciple, learning at his feet. Jesus as the sacrament of God was there before her, right in her own home, but she was not nourishing herself with his presence. What a parable about how we, too, miss out. Jesus is here, and we are elsewhere.

At the same time, this warm gathering of friends has its social-political ramifications. Society dictated that women attend to hospitality and be busy with the many things it took to keep the home fires burning. But Jesus challenged these traditional roles that persist even to our day. Jesus gently directed Martha to interrupt her distracting domestic duties, leave aside for the moment the expectations of hospitality, and instead attend to his teaching of the kin-dom of God. Whatever society says, in God's realm women also are disciples in the fullest sense.

Stories of Jesus' intimate time with his friends and his public entry into Jerusalem illustrate that following him is both a political and a private matter. In both cases, there's a choice to be made.

If we join Mary and Martha, do we choose "the better part" and sit in rapt attention with Jesus, or are we distracted by "many tasks," even when they are, in the right time, laudable tasks? Can we give up some good, respectable expectation in order to be with Jesus?

As the two Holy Week processions enter Jerusalem, we face another question: Which one do we join? That of Lord Jesus—or that of Lord Caesar, Pontius Pilate, and the collaborating religious leadership? And if we do join Jesus, do we follow this political outcast to his crucifixion? Clearly, this was a challenge that Jesus' male disciples were not up to. As the week unfurled, when the going got tough, they betrayed him, denied him, and deserted him. They failed publicly; they also failed personally. In Mark's Gospel, only a small band of brave women were there as he died on the cross (again, another strong Gospel statement on gender stereotypes).

Combined, these two stories illustrate how living sacramentally is public and personal in equal measure. Jesus incarnated the symbiotic relationship between the personal and the public, and Wesley challenged us to embrace it. "For Wesley there is no personal religion but social religion, no holiness but social holiness."[6] We aren't intended to live out our faith in a vacuum. Private acts—visiting the prisoner, serving soup in a homeless shelter, tutoring a child—are performed in the context of an unjust world. The problems of the world are overwhelming, but this is how we start to change it, one personal deed at a time. Conversely, when we take a bold public stand—as Jesus did—we're saying that, as much good as each of us can do, the world really won't be changed to benefit all unless unjust systems change. This is the conviction that can undergird and motivate our private acts, just as our private acts can inspire and motivate us to confront injustice.

Keeping our focus on the "better part," on Jesus and his way, is not easily done. There are a multitude of distractions in private life. There are a thousand reasons not to be publicly involved with a controversial kin-dom of God. Yet Jesus calls us— women and men—to transcend traditional roles and habits; he calls us to be public witnesses to God's invitation to transformation. Though Christ promises inner freedom and peace as well as citizenship in a new order, the world wants it differently. And so do some of the voices inside us. To follow Jesus and his kin-dom requires following a "narrow way," over and over allowing ourselves to be transformed in mind and heart. It calls us to be agents of God's ancient, but not yet fulfilled, promises of love, justice, and peace.

Seeking to be faithful disciples of Jesus, to center their lives on "the better part," Wesley and his movement revived religious life in England with a fresh and disciplined determination to embrace the reign of God in both its personal and public dimensions.

From his own life, Wesley knew how difficult it was to choose "the better part." He knew what it was to react irrationally when he failed in romance, to waste time on trifles, to be petrified with fear on a turbulent sea, to experience dry times in spiritual life. He knew how the powers of this world conspired to lure people away from the better part. From personal experience, he saw how people needed, in the words of the baptismal vows, to renounce, reject, resist, and repent of "evil, injustice, and oppression in whatever form they present themselves."[7]

He also knew that he—as well as the rest of us—could not do this alone. Like Wesley, we need to receive into ourselves God's "grace suffi-cient." Only with God's grace can people, like Mary of Bethany, turn their eyes upon Jesus, as the hymn goes.[8] Wesley was a methodical person—so much so that his detractors nicknamed him a "methodist." But Wesley embraced the epithet, and he nurtured followers, showing them a method for accessing God's grace and the Christian life. He called these the "works of piety" and the "works of mercy."[9] These are reliable disciplines through which we receive the "grace sufficient" to meet the challenge to walk faith-fully and justly. In this chapter, we will look at the works of piety, the reli-able "means of grace," and in the next chapter, we will examine the works of mercy that are the "fruits of grace."

WORKS OF PIETY—MEANS OF GRACE

Based on the Bible, the great spiritual writers of his time, and his personal ex-perience and observation, Wesley identified five works of piety, which he also called "windows" of grace: scripture; prayer; Christian conferencing and con-versation; Holy Communion and worship; and fasting. These are the God-ordained channels through which God places grace within the human heart, and Wesley considered them indispensable for sacramental living. Let us take a careful look at each as conduits of God's grace in our lives.

SEARCHING THE SCRIPTURES
Scripture is central to the Christian life. The key questions are how to understand these writings, and how to make them our own.[10] United Methodists have a perspective on scripture that is not necessarily shared by all Christian groups. Because this perspective is so basic to our identity and so often a matter of confusion and conflict, we will explore this work of piety in considerable depth.

For many, the act of "searching the scriptures" is discouraging, disem-powering, and even scary. Church researcher Charlene Floyd has found that many suffer from "Bible abuse." She describes how people "have difficulty negotiating theological minefields, often raising questions like, 'If I accept this [scripture], what will it mean for those I care about? Is this against women or is this against gay people?'" We know a United Methodist layman who describes himself as a "recovering Vietnam veteran," one who was severely traumatized by his war experience. What weighs on him are the recurring references in the Bible to God-sanctioned violence and wholesale slaughter.[11]

George's Story: A One-Sided Conversation

The challenge of interpreting scripture lies in the very nature of the material itself—a challenge that I would compare to listening to one side of a conversation. I recall a taxi ride I once shared with a man who talked on his cell phone almost the entire time. We were riding from the airport in Austin, Texas, and I couldn't help but overhear every word. I learned that he was a musician who was coming to Austin to perform for a night or two and then return to his home somewhere up north. I wondered who was on the other end of the conversation. His tone was warm, and he asked about the well being of others, so it had to be someone he was close to. Perhaps his mother? He concluded with, "I love you very much." Most intriguing was his reference to needing to contact a lawyer. There seemed to be some legal or financial problem in the family.

In much the same manner, when we read, say, Paul's First Letter to the Corinthians, we don't have direct access to the perspective of its recipients. In this letter, Paul seems to be quoting other people, but because quotation marks don't exist in ancient Greek, it's difficult to tell exactly which are Paul's own words and which are quotes from others. We can only infer which are his words, just as I did when I overheard the phone call.

Similarly, we have just one side of the conversation between the Gospel writers and their original audiences. Certainly, they were written to address certain questions or needs of particular groups of early Christians, each in a different region. But one must infer—from the language and content, as well as from archeological and historical evidence—what the actual issues or occasions are. Luke's Gospel, for instance, is dedicated to "most excellent Theophilus" (Luke 1:3). But who might this be? Was he a well-to-do, literate person of some importance? Or does the name Theophilus, literally "God-lover," stand for a group of would-be Jesus followers who need a comprehensive account of Jesus' life? Again, we have just one side of the conversation.

Another parallel between my musing about that taxi conversation and biblical understanding is the way both are shaped by the hearer. My assumptions about what was happening in that conversation had everything to do with my own experiences. It was quite plausible to me that he might be talking to his mother because I often ended phone conversations with my mother with similar words of affection. But he could have been speaking to his wife or someone else close to him. Also, as a native speaker of American English, I was able to understand every word this man said, including his slang. I knew, for instance, that "gig" meant a performance. I also knew, from my family's experience, that there are times when a lawyer's services are needed.

The Word of God Revealed

All of this is to explain why the words of scripture are not by themselves the word of God, but instead, they reveal the word of God through very human voices. Our Bible is really not one book, but a library of sixty-six different writings. It contains works of history (like Exodus and the Acts of the Apostles), religious and ethical instruction (Deuteronomy), social prophecy (Isaiah, Amos), prayer-poems (Psalms), wisdom literature (Proverbs) and apocalyptic accounts (Daniel, Revelation). This library also has a lot of letters (Romans, 1 and 2 Corinthians) and, most important to Christians, four Gospels (Matthew, Mark, Luke, and John). Combined, it is a unique compilation of writing that includes elements of biography, history, and faith testimony. Each literary genre in the Bible must be read with the appropriate context in mind. And just as with the taxi conversation

I was trying to comprehend, they require close attention and careful study to let the light shine from the sacred page.

The United Methodist Church maintains that this collection of writings has great authority, for "it reveals the word of God so far as it is necessary for our salvation."[12] However, these writings become authoritative for us only as they, through the power of the Holy Spirit, are responsibly interpreted. The United Methodist approach to biblical interpretation rests on what has come to be known as "The Wesleyan Quadrilateral": scripture, tradition, experience, and reason. "Wesley believed that the living core of the Christian faith was revealed in scripture, illumined by tradition, vivified in personal experience, and confirmed by reason."[13]

Further, Wesley insisted that each passage be understood in light of the "whole scope and tenor of scripture"[14]—in other words, in light of the whole sweep of biblical witness, especially the life, teaching, death, and resurrected presence of Jesus Christ. A popular tale that illustrates the importance of context tells of a man who, looking for biblical inspiration, closes his eyes, opens the New Testament, and plants his finger on what he believes will be God's direct message to him. Opening his eyes, he reads: "Throwing down the pieces of silver in the temple, [Judas] departed; and he went and hanged himself" (Matthew 27:5). That doesn't strike the man as a Christ-inspired model of behavior, so he decides to try his method again. This time, he opens his eyes and reads: "Jesus said to him, 'Go and do likewise'" (Luke 10:37). We all would reject these verses as personal admonitions because, taken literally and out of context, they certainly do not reflect the mind and heart of Jesus.

Whether in private devotion, Bible study, or preaching, several questions need to be asked of any biblical passage:

- What is going on in the world at the time, and what is the mindset of the text's author (assumptions, needs, crises, joys, anxieties)?

- What does the passage mean to the original audience for which it was composed?

- What does it mean to understand the particular passage through the mind and heart of Jesus Christ and the reign of God?

- How do our life experiences, including cultural assumptions, affect the meaning of the passage for us?

Asking such questions would have done much to mitigate the immense damage done to women on the basis of certain isolated passages attributed to Paul. In his day, the male represented full humanness, while the female was seen as fundamentally deficient and not wholly human.[15] Thus, it is all the more remarkable that the earliest church, inspired by the ministry of Jesus, boldly declared in its baptismal formula that " . . . there is no longer male and female; for all of you are one in Christ Jesus." Paul chose to live sacramentally and walk justly as he took this radical baptismal stance as his own view (Galatians 3:28).

But nevertheless, for centuries, the Christian church prevented gifted women from ordination and lay leadership on the basis of such passages as "women should be silent in the churches" (1 Corinthians 14:34), and "I permit no woman to teach or to have authority over a man; she is to keep silent" (1 Timothy 2:12). Similarly, we read that slaves "should regard their masters as worthy of all honor . . . " (1 Timothy 6:1a). But what if these passages had been seen in the context of the "whole scope and tenor" of scripture and the example of Jesus himself?

We believe that the 1 Corinthians 14:34–36 passage about women keeping silent was simply inserted by an early, unknown copyist, reflecting an increasing bias against women in leadership across the church as it faced political persecution.[16] As for the Timothy letters, there is widespread doubt about Paul's actual authorship of these and the other so-called Pastoral Epistle, the letter to Titus. They are termed "disputed letters of Paul" and give evidence of being from a later period when the church reverted to traditional Roman gender roles and master–slave relationships. Among the causes for this reversion to an outspoken patriarchal stance were the waning expectations of Christ's imminent return and the church's development from being based in homes to having a more public character.[17]

Biblical misinterpretation is hardly a vestige of the distant past—a fact we were reminded of recently during a car trip through some small towns in Pennsylvania. We came across a startling photograph in a historical society newsletter: forty hooded members of the Ku Klux Klan posing in 1923 on the front steps of the local Methodist church. We gasped. Right here? We found that little church and compared the photo to the current façade; except for the addition of a porch and windows, it looked exactly the same.

How could this congregation have provided hospitality to this violent hate group? What scriptural interpretation did they make that would allow this? Of course, we were taking in this 1923 history from a post-Civil Rights Movement perspective. But such episodes are a sober warning that biblical misinterpretation can perpetrate horrible evil in any era.

So we should read scripture with a critical eye, alert to the reality that enduring truth is often obscured by the unchristlike customs and vocabulary of the times. But we do not just question scripture; we should also let scripture question us and raise issues about our values, practices, and concern for our neighbor.

The Book of Discipline of The United Methodist Church explains the church's approach to scripture in this way:

> We interpret individual texts in light of their place in the Bible as a whole. We are aided by scholarly inquiry and personal insight, under the guidance of the Holy Spirit. As we work with scripture, we take into account what we have been able to learn about the original context and intention of the text. In this understanding, we draw upon the careful historical, literary, and textual studies in recent years that have enriched our understanding of the Bible.

> Through this faithful reading of Scripture, we may come to know the truth of the biblical message in its bearing on our own lives and the life of the world. Thus, the Bible [as a whole] serves both as a

source of our faith and as the basic criterion by which the truth and fidelity of any interpretation [of a particular passage] is measured.[18]

PRAYER

By their very nature, the sacraments point to how much God wants to communicate with us and invite us into a relationship. When we pray, we are opening ourselves up to God, creating the possibility of being swept off our feet by a great life-changing flood of grace. Prayer allows us to share our deepest yearnings for the reign of God in our lives and in society; it is how we can seek to align our hearts with the heart of God and the mind of Christ. Wesley strongly endorsed Paul's encouragement to the Thessalonians: "Rejoice always, pray without ceasing. . . ." (1 Thessalonians 5:16–17). Yet prayer also is a mysterious act that can make many of us feel uncomfortable, perplexed, and daunted before we even begin.

A prison inmate once asked me (Tilda), "So, how am I supposed to pray? What do I do?" What a beautiful question, so full of longing and possibility! And how challenging it was to respond simply.

Part of the answer lies in asking God to shape our prayers, then sinking down into the truest part of ourselves—to that place where we are naked, honest, and thirsty. There we may find words of confession, praise, or inquiry. But we must also be prepared to find some unwanted words of doubt, fear, cynicism, lust, or even rage. We can let these be. After all, we did ask God to be in charge.

Perhaps our words are traditional. They could be a portion of scripture, the Lord's Prayer, or another liturgical prayer of the church. We may have no words at all—just a welcome into God's presence, an invitation for us to be still and let God love us while we love God back.

Then we can pay attention to what happens next. Perhaps we will feel a memory surface or see an image of a person in our lives. Maybe we will feel a nudge to make a phone call or to take some other action. Before we dismiss this as a distraction, we can also remember that sometimes this is how God speaks. Perhaps we will sense that God wants to heal something in us or draw us to deeper honesty. As we pray, we can ask God to bring forward what is important and let the rest fade.

How do we know if we've received a divine message? Evaluation, or discernment, is crucial. None of us perceives God's communication infallibly, and most of us are quite capable of constructing a rosy picture spun of moonbeams. After you pray is the time to ask yourself: Was my prayer full of God or just full of me? Am I insisting that my prayer be answered in a particular way? Am I holding on to old pain, old habits, or old stories because they feel safer than risking change? Am I trying to get God to be a magician on my personal payroll? This is also the time to ask God to keep correcting you until you get it right and then trust that God will honor your desire to hear and follow.

Christian prayer is not always easy, and many obstacles can get in the way: a hectic schedule, fatigue, illness, our own ambitions and appetites. Social prejudice or structures can grind people down and drive them away from prayer, or paradoxically, they can be an impetus to a prayerful discovery that God is present in suffering. The death of a loved one or other tragedy can generate anger and despair. But it also may be when we realize through prayer that nothing can separate us from the love of Christ (Romans 8:38–39).

Charlene Floyd tells the story of Debra Pressley of Charlotte, Virginia, who had a problem with prayer after her seventeen-year-old son, Ryan, was killed in a car accident a few blocks from home. "She has heard many people say 'this sickness or that illness was healed because of my prayers' or 'our prayers saved him.' It hurts her to hear that because, she says, 'We prayed just as much, we loved our child just as much . . . .'"[19]

There are no glib answers to Pressley's cry of the heart, nor to ours. Pressley did not give up praying. "I try real hard at it," she said. "I do more of a dialogue thing, which I think is prayer, too. . . . I do have a constant dialogue with God all the time. And I think of that as prayer. . . .So I pray, but it's probably not the conventional [way]."[20]

Despite Pressley's uncertainty, her prayer still rings with raw honesty, akin to the "praying without ceasing" that the Apostle Paul urged and

Wesley embraced. She is finding her way, and we can hope that someday she will be able to speak powerfully about an inner peace that makes absolutely no sense, the peace that "passes all understanding." She may become a person others look to for companionship in hard times. Her suffering will have been transformed, or redeemed, into a well of gift and grace for herself and others.

Pressley's story illustrates how prayer is a process that ushers lifelong growth and healing. Whenever we are in communication with God, we can trust that we will be changed somehow.

CHRISTIAN CONFERENCING AND CONVERSATION

When we think about church meetings, we may recollect experiences that were grace filled, alive with possibility, joy, and creativity. Something happened that changed things for the better. But just as likely, we may remember the meetings that were dry and deadening. Perhaps someone in the room dominated, while others could hardly get a word in. We may have witnessed expressions of cynicism, defeatism, exclusivity, stinginess, or unwillingness to try something new.

Wesley said that Christian conferencing was a means of grace, a window for further growth in God. He must have had that first kind of meeting in mind. In such meetings, as in grace-filled conversations, we offer one another a listening ear, encouragement, mutual accountability, and support for living of the faith.

Some years ago, researcher Charles Olson discovered that when lay people quit serving on their local church's governing body, a high proportion reported being dissatisfied. The most common disappointment was the lack of spiritual community. Their meetings more closely resembled a typically boring or abrasive civic or business meeting rather than the spiritual experience they had anticipated. This researcher took a constructive approach, however. Olson also closely examined churches where, in contrast, board meetings were positive spiritual experiences—means of grace—and, gleaning from their stories, he put together a guide for church boards.[21]

According to Olson, the elements of such meetings include:

- sharing faith stories by participants,
- weaving together the ongoing story of the congregation with biblical stories,
- deliberately practicing discernment, and
- surrounding the meeting with prayer.

For example, rather than have "bookend prayers" at the beginning and end, he suggested that prayer be spread throughout the meeting. Another idea involved asking various participants to each monitor a different agenda item, then be prepared to offer a sentence prayer for that particular concern as part of a collective closing prayer.[22]

Wesley surely would have endorsed such an approach, for he believed that the gathering of Christians to confer and to converse about matters of the Spirit could be a powerful means of grace. A familiar hymn calls to mind the spirit of such gatherings:

> Blest be the tie that binds our hearts in Christian love;
> the fellowship of kindred hearts is like to that above. . .
>
> We share each other's woes, our mutual burdens bear; and often for
> each other flows the sympathizing tear.[23]

Christian conferencing and conversation take many forms, including "spiritual friendship."[24] Two persons covenant to regularly spend time with each other—time that's dedicated to frank sharing about life and faith. Spiritual friendship may also happen in groups where matters of faith are shared in some depth, such as United Methodist Women organizations and spiritual growth gatherings. One way to begin a time of spiritual friendship is to respond to a question: What "God moments" have you experienced recently? Or, how is God at work in your life?

Another entry point for Christian conversation is through devotional material. In this way, we are able to think along with an author or presenter and create our own dialogue around questions of Christian faith and action. The United Methodist Women magazine **response** is a rich resource for long-distance Christian conversation. Each monthly issue is packed with opportunities to walk with new and old United Methodist Women friends in sections such as "Think," "Learn," "Live," "Give," "Listen," "Act," and "Pray." United Methodist Women colleagues can also connect through the UMWOnline Community and United Methodist Women social media links. The United Methodist-sponsored Upper Room Ministries has three excellent publications to befriend: *The Upper Room* daily devotional guide and two bimonthly magazines, *Alive Now* and *Weavings: A Journal of the Christian Spiritual Life.*

In recent years, the tensions within The United Methodist Church over differing theological perspectives have received special attention. Various church bodies have worked to foster a spirit of unity in diversity. Out of this conversation has grown recommendations for "holy conferencing," based on Colossians 3:12–17, that are intended for use at annual conferences and the General Conference, as well as any time United Methodists gather to confer:

- Every person is a child of God. Always speak respectfully. One can disagree without being disagreeable.

- As you patiently listen and observe the behavior of others, be open to the possibility that God can change the views of any or all parties in the discussion.

- Listen patiently before formulating responses.

- Strive to understand the experience out of which others have arrived at their views.

- Be careful in how you express personal offense at differing opinions. Otherwise, dialogue may be inhibited.

- Accurately reflect the views of others when speaking. This is especially important when you disagree with that position.

- Avoid using inflammatory words, derogatory names, or an excited and angry voice.

- Avoid making generalizations about individuals and groups. Make your point with specific evidence and examples.

- Make use of facilitators and mediators.

- Remember that people are defined, ultimately, by their relationship with God—not by the flaws we discover, or think we discover, in their views and actions.[25]

HOLY COMMUNION AND WORSHIP

In the previous chapter, we discussed the many ways in which Holy Communion may be a special means of God's grace. For Wesley, the Eucharist was the central experience of Christian worship, but he also encouraged his followers to join in regular corporate worship in a variety of forms. As Tilda's intimate experiences with the Eucharist illustrate, corporate worship isn't necessary to participate in this sacrament. Still, Wesley placed a special emphasis on the communal quality of Communion.

In this era of dwindling church membership and attendance, many people are obviously questioning the importance of corporate worship. Indeed, it is possible and commendable to worship alone, but no one can be a church of one. Jesus stressed his presence in the gathered community: "For where two or three are gathered in my name, I am there among them" (Matthew 18:20). And Paul stressed that the church is the body of Christ, made up of many members, each with special gifts (1 Corinthians 12:4–31). Experience confirms that we need one another for support, encouragement, sharing wisdom and knowledge, inspiration, and ministry projects that can't be done alone. We need a place to offer our own gifts to build up the body of Christ. We need to help nourish new members and support those who are going through deep waters. We need to sing together, join our voices in prayer, and gather around the table of the Lord.

But as holy as church is intended to be, it is made up of human beings, and humanity's shortcomings don't stop at its doors. Like families, some churches are full of dissension or power brokering. Some have lost their nerve and consistently take the safe way in every decision. Others have settled into bland, poorly planned worship, lackluster music, or preaching that lacks originality and inspiration. If this is true of your church, perhaps there is a decision ahead of you: to stay and lovingly support what is good and work hard for change, or shake the dust off your feet and move on to another congregation. We suggest that this decision not be made hastily, but with much prayer and careful discernment, taking the time to admit both your needs and your own part in the problem.

If your church is not nourishing you as much as you want or if you long for more depth in worship, here are actions you can take, short of leaving:

- Check out what other churches in your neighborhood are doing. Are there special or occasional services that might feed you? Are there special ecumenical celebrations in your area? Is there a retreat center or campus ministry nearby that offers creative worship? Is there a monastery that invites outsiders to sit in silence with the monastics?

- Try attending daily Eucharist services in a church that offers it.

- Attend United Methodist Women events and retreats.

- Invite a few like-minded folks to meet at your house from time to time to worship together. Turn to *The United Methodist Hymnal* for orders of evening or morning prayer.[26] Experiment with a Love Feast, a renewal of baptismal vows, or a service of prayer and anointing. See what happens if you gather to prayerfully wash one another's feet. You don't necessarily need a pastor for any of this, but your pastor might enjoy joining you or helping with planning.

- Create a personal liturgy for the benefit of just one person. You might celebrate a milestone with friends, bless a job change or some important growth, assist in a process of forgiveness, or provide a setting in which to surrender destructive patterns and embrace something new. For example, in my ministry I (Tilda) have helped create a liturgy for a woman who wanted to celebrate her recovery from cancer with her pastor and some church friends.

■ A colleague worked with a teenager who requested a liturgy to celebrate earning her driver's license. She recited vows to drive safely, and two of her good friends vowed to support her in her new responsibility. Another liturgy addressed the hopelessness of a woman who had experienced the tragic death of her children and her husband's subsequent abandonment. She created a "garden of hope" with her friends. It was an actual garden in a desolate vacant lot to symbolize both her despair and her trust that somehow God was planting seeds of healing. As time went on, church friends frequently stopped by the garden to pray for her healing. As the garden bloomed, so did her hope.[27]

The possibilities for creative worship are endless. All that is required is initiative and a sense of adventure with God.

FASTING

As Methodist historian Charles Yrigoyen points out, "When most of us think about fasting, it is usually because it is time to lose some weight. When Wesley thought about it, he viewed it as a spiritual discipline whose purpose was not to reduce the intake of calories but to enhance the holy life."[28] Wesley saw fasting as a means of grace, a way of focusing more centrally on God, and a method of providing the impetus to take an inventory of our spiritual lives.

When we consider fasting, we may want to think about giving up certain self-indulgences, besides food, that stand in the way of our God-consciousness and our ethical behavior. For example, think of yourself in relation to how you watch television, use the Internet and social media, or spend money. What behavior do you know you should curb? For some, this form of sacramental living may mean changing routines that prevent adequate sleep. Certainly, weariness undermines our best intentions to be attentive to the presence of God in our interior, interpersonal, and public lives.

New York Times technology columnist Nick Bilton shares his self-imposed challenge:

> Last week, I drove to Pacifica, a beach community just south of San Francisco, where I climbed a large rocky hill as the sun descended on the horizon. It painted a typically astounding California sunset across the Pacific Ocean. What did I do next?
>
> What any normal person would do in 2011: I pulled out my iPhone and began snapping pictures to share on Instagram, Facebook and Twitter. I spent 10 minutes trying to compose the perfect shot. . . . Then I stopped. Here I was, watching this magnificent sunset, and all I could do is peer at it through a tiny four-inch screen.
>
> "What's wrong with me?" I thought. "I can't seem to enjoy anything without trying to digitally capture it or spew it onto the Internet." Hence my New Year's resolution: In 2012, I plan to spend at least 30 minutes a day without my iPhone. Without Internet, Twitter, Facebook and my iPad."[29]

Bilton's problem may be somewhat extreme and his resolve rather modest, but all of us can relate to the problem of habits and attitudes that shield us from God's real presence in life and creation. The frontier for us might be to begin to let go, by the grace of God, of resentment or pessimism, negativity or fear.

Besides abstaining from personal indulgences and attitudes, however, we suggest taking a further step and consider giving up products or services that are associated with human and environmental exploitation. For instance, you might take public transportation rather than drive or avoid disposable water bottles in favor of refillable containers. Let living sacramentally include walking justly—in very concrete lifestyle choices.

It is common for us to ask one another, "What are you giving up for Lent?" But in recent times, people have been encouraged to ask themselves about what they are going to take on for Lent. In other words, what special discipline might we add to our lives to express our love of God and one another in some extraordinary way? This could mean driving a neighbor to the doctor or making a generous donation to an action group that addresses the causes of poverty and growing imbalance in wealth. It could also mean a vow to frequently sign petitions and send messages to public figures that reflect the prophet Micah's urging "to do justice, and to love kindness, and to walk humbly with your God" (Micah 6:8). Or, to take an all-too-rare approach, we might send messages of support to public figures who are speaking out for justice. Choosing creative ways to make a difference is, in fact, a form of fasting from our own indifference. [30]

We invite you to explore more intentionally how fasting may be a means of grace for you. As you become aware of what you are letting go of, let that sensation prompt a new dimension of trust in God for "grace sufficient" in this and every part of your life.

HOW TO APPROACH BIBLE STUDY

A variety of resources can be used in private devotion or in a group. Many United Methodists have learned much about the Bible and deepened their faith through *Disciple Bible Study*.[31] United Methodist Women mission studies include excellent guides for Bible study, such the 2010 spiritual growth study, *For the Love of God: The Epistles of John* by the wife–husband team of Catherine and Justo Gonzalez.[32] For Lenten study, one cannot do better than *The Last Week*, a day-by-day study of Jesus' last days by preeminent New Testament scholars Marcus Borg and John Dominic Crossan.[33] For Advent and Christmas, *The Liberation of Christmas* is an excellent resource.[34]

More challenging to read, but most rewarding, is *In Search of Paul: How Jesus's Apostle Opposed Rome's Empire with God's Kingdom* by Crossan and archeologist Jonathan Reed. To explore issues of biblical interpretation through reading a novel, we recommend *Putting Away Childish Things* by Marcus Borg.[35]

Another approach to study is to read a commentary along with the Bible. You can find a short commentary from a woman's perspective on each book of the Bible in *The Women's Bible Commentary*, edited by Carol A. Newsom and Sharon H. Ringe, both of whom teach at United Methodist seminaries. The *For Everyone Bible Study Guides* by N. T. Wright, an Anglican bishop, are exceptionally readable and well informed.[36] United Methodism's Abingdon Press publishes excellent standard reference works that you may find in a pastor's or church library, such as *The New Interpreter's Bible* (twelve volumes), *The New Interpreter's Dictionary of the Bible* (five volumes), and *The New Interpreter's Bible One-Volume Commentary*.

Reenactment-style Bible study, in which group members simulate the roles of early church members, offers a creative approach to scriptural understanding. One notable example of this genre is Reta Halteman Finger's *Roman House Churches for Today*.[37] Finger and George McClain have teamed up to write an upcoming reenactment study of 1 Corinthians, which will be published by Mennomedia.

HOW TO ENRICH YOUR PRAYER LIFE

■ Link your prayer to world news. Nurture in yourself the mind of Christ (Philippians 2:5) as you read a news story or watch a news report. Pray for victims of cruelty and abuse. Where there is conflict and disregard for human life, pray for peace. Where there is great wealth amassed through exploitation and the violation of trust, pray for justice. Call to mind the canticle of Mary, that God "has scattered the proud in the imagination of their hearts . . . and lifted up the lowly . . . and sent the rich away empty" (Luke 1:46–55). Ask if there is a way God wants you to act in response. Theologian Karl Barth declared that "to clasp the hands in prayer is the beginning of an uprising against the disorder of the world."[38]

■ Try a day—or more—of silence in which you are alone with God. This is best done away from home where there is no to-do list glowering at you. Go to a retreat center, camp in a nature preserve, or borrow someone's weekend place.

■ Try *lectio divina,* which literally means "divine reading." This is a slow, deliberate reading of a small portion of scripture or devotional text. Breathe into every word. Pay attention to what shines out at you. Let prayer flow from your reading.

■ Pray with music. Sing along with hymns, and let them express your prayer. Listen to what God might be communicating. An excellent resource is the music of the Taizé ecumenical monastic community in France.

■ Try faith-imagination prayer. Invite God to enter into your awareness in a way that you can imaginatively perceive. Offer to God your capacity for inner seeing, hearing, sensing, and knowing. Perhaps you will "see" images of God or Jesus, or "hear" something with your mind's ear. Or you may simply sense the presence of God, and that sensing will be full of meaning. Or you might become aware of a new idea that changes everything.

Trust that God will communicate in a way that reaches you. Try not to toss anything out until you have had the chance to reflect on it later. If nothing occurs to you, remember you can't control God, and try again another day.[39]

HOW TO READ SCRIPTURE FAITHFULLY

Take the scriptures seriously, not literally.

Recognize the humanity of the biblical authors: All fashioned their writing with specific contemporary issues and audiences in mind. Try to imagine how their audiences heard their messages. Recognize that the perfect word of God is accessible to us only through the witness of imperfect human beings. Though they had remarkable experiences and encounters with God, their world-views were quite different from ours.

Try reading scripture from the perspective of the poor, marginalized, and forgotten. Let that include the more vulnerable and impoverished parts of yourself. In your imagination, invite the silent ones in scripture to find their voice. For instance:

- What might the feisty Corinthian women prophets have to say about being ranked below men ("woman is a reflection of man") and being told to wear their hair in a particular way (1 Corinthians 11:2–16)?
- What would slaves say about being in bondage to a Christian master?[40]
- What can Phoebe tell us about her part in Paul's ministry? (Romans 16:1-2) For instance, does she underwrite his journeys? Does he travel on her ships?
- When the psalmist cries out, "Incline your ear to me; rescue me speedily. Be a rock of refuge for me . . . . " (Psalm 31:2),

what is he or she experiencing? Physical suffering, depression, family illness, hunger, poverty?

■ When the crowds hear Jesus declare the Beatitudes, what do they think? For instance, when he says, "Blessed are those who mourn, for they shall be comforted" (Matthew 5:4), do they shed tears and think of all their babies and children who died so young? Do they relive their powerlessness as their daughters and sons were raped by Roman soldiers?

Because each of us brings very different experiences to scripture, we can't expect everyone to understand a particular passage in the same way. There is often so much in a passage, and on so many levels, that there can be no single interpretation. But as we share our interpretations with one another, we each gain a deeper appreciation of the power of God's Word as it radiates from the words of the Bible.

As you question scripture, let the Holy Spirit question you about your life and faith. Let there be a dialogue. While we may question Paul, for instance, about why he's so concerned about women's hair, let us also let him question us about how we may better fashion our lives so faith, hope, and love are what matter most (1 Corinthians 13:13).

Finally, allow a certain joy to be a part of your study. Jesus himself was full of joy and fun and loved parties and meals with friends.[41] As one woman told author Charlene Floyd, "The Bible is so good with chocolate. I always thought the Bible was more of a salad thing, you know, but it isn't. It's a chocolate thing."[42] So revel in the Bible; gorge on it. Allow it to challenge you, to comfort you, and to awaken a sense of mystery. Open your heart to surprising discoveries in these ancient holy texts.

HOW TO PRAY FOR CHRISTIAN CONFERENCING

The following is a method of praying for meetings, gatherings, and events so that they can be channels of grace.[43]

If you are able, go to the site of the gathering ahead of time to pray. Invite another person or two to join you. If not, pray by yourself or in another place, imagining the space and the participants as best you can.

■ Pray that the meeting space and the hearts of the participants be cleared of anything that would interfere with the Holy Spirit.

■ Imagine God's presence as a light, a breeze, or a gentle sound enveloping the entire space and those who will be present.

■ Move about the space reverently, sitting or standing in the places participants will be occupying, inviting God's active presence in each. Include prayer for the events that will unfold: the agenda, the decisions, the conversation, perhaps the sharing of food and drink.

■ Thank God in advance for the divine presence in the event, then be at prayer even as you participate.

---

1   Marcus J. Borg and John Dominic Crossan, *The Last Week: What the Gospels Really Teach About Jesus's Final Days in Jerusalem* (New York: HarperCollins, 2006), 1ff.

2   Ibid., 2.

3   Ibid., 8.

4   "A Service of Word and Table I," *The United Methodist Hymnal,* (Nashville, Abingdon Press, 1993), 10.

5   Ibid.

6   *The Book of Discipline of The United Methodist Church 2008* (Nashville: Abingdon Press, 2008), ¶48.

7   "Congregational Reaffirmation of the Baptismal Covenant," *The United Methodist Hymnal* (Nashville, The United Methodist Publishing House, 1993), 50.

8   "Turn Your Eyes Upon Jesus," *The United Methodist Hymnal,* 349.

9   Charles Yrigoyen, Jr.'s *John Wesley: Holiness of Heart and Life* is an excellent introduction to Wesley's theology.

10 The special term for this type of study is "biblical hermeneutics," or how the Bible is interpreted.

11 George D. McClain, *Claiming All Things for God: Prayer, Discernment, and Ritual for Social Change* (Nashville: Abingdon Press, 1998), 50. Contains a chapter on "The Crisis in Biblical Authority," 48ff.

12 "Articles of Religion of the Methodist Church," *The Book of Discipline,* ¶67.

13 *The Book of Discipline,* ¶77.

14 *The Works of John Wesley,* Volume 3, Sermons III (Nashville: Abingdon Press, 1986, 522, Sermon, "Free Grace" (1739) section 20.

15 Dale B. Martin, *The Corinthian Body* (New Haven and London: Yale University Press, 1995).

16 Note that because of the uncertainty of Paul's authorship, 1 Corinthians 14:33b–36 is placed in parentheses in the New Revised Standard Version of the New Testament. Note also how the chapter flows so much more logically without the interpolated verses about women's silence and subordination.

17 Bart D. Ehrman, *The New Testament: A Historical Introduction to the Early Christian Writings,* (New York, Oxford: Oxford University Press, 2008), 403–415.

18 *The Book of Discipline,* ¶78–79.

19 Floyd, *Christian Voices,* 19.

20 Ibid., 18.

21 Charles M. Olsen, *Transforming Church Boards into Communities of Spiritual Leaders* (An Alban Institute Publication, 1995).

22 Ibid., 20–21.

23 "Blest Be the Tie that Binds," *The United Methodist Hymnal,* 557.

24 Tilden Edwards, *Spiritual Friend: Reclaiming the Gift of Spiritual Direction* (Mahwah, NJ: Paulist Press, 1980).

25 These "Guidelines for Holy Conferencing—What God Expects from Us" can be found in downloadable PDF form at www.umc.org/atf/cf/%7Bdb6a45e4-c446-4248-82c8-e131b6424741%7D/GUIDELINESFORCHRISTIANCONFERENCING5.PDF,

26 "Orders of Daily Praise and Prayer," *The United Methodist Hymnal,* 876–879.

27 For more ideas and help, see Tilda Norberg, *Gathered Together: Creating Personal Liturgies for Healing and Transformation* (Nashville: Upper Room Books, 2007).

28 Charles Yrigoyen, Jr., *John Wesley: Holiness of Heart and Life* (Nashville: Abingdon Press, 1996), with study guide by Ruth A. Daugherty, 46–47.

29 Nick Bilton, "Resolving to Practice Some iPhone Abstinence," *New York Times,* January 2, 2012, B3.

30 The websites of the United Methodist Women (www.unitedmethodistwomen.
    org) and the United Methodist General Board of Church and Society (www.umc-
    gbcs.org) offer frequent suggestions for action in keeping with United Methodist
    social teaching.

31 Nancy Kruh, *The Disciple Story: The Transforming Power of Scripture* (Nashville:
    Abingdon Press, 2003).

32 Catherine Gunsalus Gonzalez and Justo L. Gonzalez, *For the Love of God: The
    Epistles of John* (New York: United Methodist Women, 2010).

33 Marcus J. Borg and John Dominic Crossan, *The Last Week: What the Gospels Really
    Teach About Jesus's Final Days in Jerusalem* (New York: HarperCollins, 2006).

34 Richard A. Horsley, *The Liberation of Christmas: The Infancy Narratives in Social
    Context* (New York: Crossroad Publishing Company, 1989).

35 Marcus J. Borg, *Putting Away Childish Things: A Tale of Modern Faith* (New York:
    HarperOne, 2010).

36 Available for many New Testament books from Westminster John Knox Press.

37 Reta Haltman Finger, *Roman House Churches for Today: A Practical Guide for Small
    Groups* (Grand Rapids, MI: William B. Eerdmanns Publishing Company, 2007).

38 Goodreads, "Quotes by Karl Barth," accessed July 1, 2012, www.goodreads.com/
    author/show/23117.Karl_Barth.

39 For more information on faith-imagination prayer, see Tilda Norberg, *Consenting
    to Grace: An Introduction to Gestalt Pastoral Care* (Staten Island, NY: Penn House
    Press, 2006), 57–71.

40 See, for instance, Paul's *Letter to Philemon.*

41 See James Martin, *Between Heaven and Mirth: Why Joy, Humor, and Laughter Are
    at the Heart of the Spiritual Life* (New York: HarperOne, 2011).

42 Floyd, *Christian Voices,* 153.

43 Adapted from George McClain's *Claiming All Things for God,* where additional
    suggestions can be found.

CHAPTER 3

Doing God's Work in the World

By George McClain and Tilda Norberg

A PARABLE: A ROAD TO THE FUTURE

Once upon a time there was a village in a mountain valley, with only one way in and out. The road through the mountains dated back to early times when people walked or traveled by horse and cart. It had since been paved over for motor vehicles, but it had the same narrow, dangerous curves and steep grades.

As you could imagine, many accidents occurred along this road, especially in icy weather. Naturally, the community had a great concern about the victims, and the village fathers and mothers continually spoke about the importance of stopping and caring for the injured. When clergy preached on the story of the Good Samaritan, they held this ideal high and warmly commended those who tended to the injured and brought them to the village hospital.

Out of this concern, the villagers got the idea of having an ambulance available at any moment to rescue the traffic victims. Although some wondered whether that was really necessary, the village rallied around the idea, established a volunteer ambulance service, and supported it with donations and fundraisers. The local clergy lauded the new service as institutionalized Good Samaritan-ship. The ambulance vehicle was even named "The Good Samaritan."

Critics, however, noted that, even though aid was getting to the injured more efficiently, the rate of injury was unchanged. Other citizens raised fears that the road's condition could cause a disaster. Though no one had been killed on this stretch of road, vocal activists warned that it was just a matter of time. At first dismissed as negativists and alarmists, these watchdogs kept citing the facts and insisting, quite emotionally, that something had *to be done about this dangerous road.*

Despite considerable resistance, concerned citizens finally were able to initiate a public conversation: neighborhood and community meetings were held to weigh the pros and cons of road improvement, and the topic became much discussed among friends and families. Meanwhile, more statistics were marshaled and experts in traffic safety were consulted. Some taxpayers argued against doing anything major because of the enormous cost —money that could be spent on many other community needs. They instead proposed erecting more warning signs. Some said the accidents were the victims' own fault for driving recklessly. Others argued that the road was a historic treasure that had served the village well for centuries. The business community stressed that a new, modern road would bring prosperity to the village. Churchwomen and youth campaigned for a new road, going door-to-door to promote "A Road to the Future."

There was a tense period of wrangling, and over time, the village seemed to settle into a stalemate. Then the news came: a van of seniors on an excursion had swerved sharply to avoid a fallen rock and had almost gone over a cliff. Three passengers had to be hospitalized, and one almost died.

The women and children and youth intensified their campaign, pleading on people's doorsteps for a spirit of compassion, sacrifice, and concern for present and future generations. Eventually, a large majority agreed that major improvements must be made. Although the state would pitch in significant funds, the plan would still require a local tax increase. But with grassroots support and village opinion-makers lending leadership, the local government reached the decision to reconstruct the whole road.

Elected officials prepared the community for years-long inconvenience during construction, but at the same time, they celebrated the willingness of the village to undertake a "radical" approach that addressed the underlying problem at its roots. In sermons, local clergy declared that the early proponents of road reconstruction were "today's prophets."

Our questions for you are the following: Where do you see yourself in this story? If you had been there, in what role would you have felt most comfortable? Stopping to rescue the victims, or relying on someone else to get involved? Volunteering for the ambulance corps? Campaigning early on for a "radical" solution? Warning about a future catastrophe? Worrying about the cost of a new road? Campaigning door-to-door for "A Road to the Future"? Demanding to hear from outside experts? Taking a leadership role to look for a compromise? Calling for calm and rational discussion? Or, for whatever reason, not feeling a need to get involved at all?

We're all capable of a wide variety of responses to pressing issues, whether personal, local, or global. Some of us like to act quickly and decisively, others prefer to be more deliberate. Some of us want to be "hands on" with the people affected, while others feel more motivated to take the case to leaders and try to change public policy. Sometimes we seek a compromise. Sometimes we do nothing and trust time to take its course.

Though the story of the road is a parable, all of us have faced countless opportunities in our lives to reach out to others in times of need. When we do, we are responding to the call to perform what John Wesley called "works of mercy." Arising from the stirring of God's grace within us, these works show themselves as outward expressions of compassion, justice, peace, and reconciliation. Being filled with the presence of Christ at the Lord's Table, we take seriously our Communion prayer, "that we may be for the world the body of Christ."[1] We exercise the ministry of Christ to which we have been commissioned in our baptism. In these acts, we cooperate with God in the divine healing and care of God's children and God's creation—sometimes with those near to us and sometimes with those we'll never know.

In the previous chapter, we discussed the works of piety that cultivate the means of grace. For Wesley, sacramental living does not stop there but expresses itself in works of mercy. As Charles Yrigoyen reminds us, Wesley vehemently maintained that faith without works of love and justice (James 2:14–26) is "the grand pest of Christianity."[2] According to Wesley, the works of mercy are:

> . . . feeding the hungry, . . . clothing the naked, . . . entertaining or assisting the stranger, . . . visiting those that are sick or in prison, . . . comforting the afflicted, . . . instructing the ignorant, . . . reproving the wicked, . . . exhorting and encouraging the well-doer; and . . . any other work of mercy.[3]

In this chapter, we shall examine the variety of ways in which Christians perform these works of mercy in our time; then we will explore how God's call comes to us to join in the divine initiative of healing the brokenness of the world.

Let's take a close look at the different ways we engage in works of mercy that respond to human need, especially in relation to the needs of neighbors beyond our immediate circle. In doing so, we will refer to the road reconstruction parable and the example of Wesley, as well as to contemporary life. We will also emphasize how these works of mercy, springing as they do out of God's grace, are, or should be, transformational. They unleash power that changes things and moves us in the direction of the kin-dom of God.

DIRECT, ONE-TO-ONE AID[4]

The people in our parable—those who saw victims along the road and stopped to help them—acted with one-to-one compassion, perhaps at some inconvenience or risk to themselves just like the Good Samaritan of Luke's Gospel (Luke 10:25–37). Wesley and the early Methodists visited the sick, counseled the imprisoned, gave food to the hungry, and rode in the cart with the condemned on the way to the gallows. Each of us likely offers frequent personal care and love to friends and family. We lend a listening ear, drive someone to the doctor's office, volunteer to babysit, pick up children from school, or help out with money.

Opportunities in our path can sometimes lead to extraordinary and unexpected outcomes. A friend of ours, whose mother died twenty years ago while waiting for a liver transplant, was visiting a hospital intensive care unit and fell into conversation with a woman mourning a friend who was brain-dead. She told her mother's story to the acquaintance, and as a result, she learned the next day that the family had decided to donate their loved one's organs so that others might have the gift of life.

In providing direct help, we follow in the footsteps of the early Methodists who founded orphanages, clinics, and schools to meet glaring needs. Much of our denomination's community outreach today occurs through projects, programs, and institutions that enable us to unite with others around a common goal.

Frequently this happens through our congregations. Church initiatives can be as tender and intimate as the Prayers and Squares group at St. John's United Methodist Church in Lugoff, South Carolina. The group creates quilts that are prayed over and then distributed, mostly to the sick and frequently to those outside the church. Group members compare what they do to a constant laying on of hands.[5]

Or an initiative can be as intense and all encompassing as the Open Table, a nonprofit started at Paradise Valley United Methodist Church in Arizona by layman Jon Katov. Open Table arranges for a group of dedicated volunteers to meet over time with a person who is seeking to be liberated from a cycle of poverty. Participants offer emotional and spiritual support, arrange for postponed medical and dental care, and help out with any legal entanglements. Pooling their resources and connections, they offer what they call "a lifeboat for those on the margins of society."[6]

Such one-to-one acts of compassion can be occasions of transformation, not only for the recipient, but also for the givers. Campus minister Rob Rynders, who coordinates an Open Table program at Arizona State's Wesley Foundation, states that wrestling with the realities of a poor person's life is "not an easy thing. It rearranges your molecules, and it hurts sometimes." But he welcomes "the work that God does in your heart" through such an encounter. God joins with the caregiver "to change how you see the world, how you see poverty . . . ," he says. "It sends good ripples through the rest of your ministry about what your priorities are." Charles Shock, an attorney who participates in Open Table, comments, "Sometimes God stretches us in ways we are not exactly sure of. Sometimes when you do take that leap and you don't know exactly where you are leaping, it can be very fulfilling."[7]

Among local churches, organizing direct aid is often simply a part of who they are. An untold number of congregations count among their ministries a food pantry, clothing depot, homeless shelter, scholarship committee, and community garden. Many churches sponsor mission trips, going into communities to build homes and churches, often in the wake of natural disasters. After this personal contact with human need, their common refrain is that their involvement has transformed them.

We personally experienced such transformation through the theological study program we organized in prison. Some evenings, we would drag ourselves into the prison facility for our weekly seminars and, in our fatigue, wonder why we were doing this. But invariably, we found ourselves blessed by our contact with the men inside. Their courage, faith, vulnerability, and desire to make amends would touch us with God's grace. And when we left later in the evening, we found ourselves newly energized and refreshed in spirit. We continue to be dogged by the question: what can we do to help them make a successful transition as contributing members of society?

EDUCATION, CONVERSATION, MOTIVATION

In our parable, the traffic-safety watchdogs studied the problem, marshaled the relevant statistics, and laid the facts before the community—in effect, they developed an educational campaign. They also organized neighborhood meetings where a community conversation could be launched. The churchwomen and youth who initiated the "Road to the Future" campaign created powerful motivation for change when they knocked on doors and asked whether people would join them to reduce the accident rate.

One of Wesley's truly creative acts in reaching out to transform lives through education was to gather and publish the best medical wisdom of the day in a book called *Primitive Physick; or An Easy and Natural Method of Curing Most Diseases,* which today we might simply entitle "Basic Medicine." He wanted to acquaint those without access to any professional care with knowledge of health practices, herbal medicines, and home remedies they could use on their own.

A current example is United Methodist Women's efforts to make an impact on human trafficking, the fastest growing criminal industry in the world today. Its victims are those who live and toil under coercion or fraud, usually in conditions hardly above slavery. Because such activity is especially pronounced around large entertainment events, United Methodist Women partnered with other groups in an Intercept Human Trafficking educational campaign for the 2012 Super Bowl in Indianapolis. Organizers created fliers, postcards, and worship bulletins, emphasizing the prevalence of forced labor in service industries, and distributed them to churches, local stores, community centers, meetings, and private parties.[8]

The work of mission education and motivation can be enhanced by a work of mercy that Katie Day, a seminary professor and church researcher, calls "difficult conversations."[9] Such conversations offer a way to address important matters that may be controversial or potentially divisive. She believes that engaging in such conversations actually strengthens congregations, communities, and even families. Done with mutual respect and careful advanced planning, they can become examples of the Christian conversation or holy conferencing discussed in the previous chapter as one of Wesley's means of grace.

One key to enabling constructive conversations across cultural and religious divides is Day's admonition to "let judgment become curiosity." Rather than rush to a negative judgment about what seems strange, new, or even offensive to us, she counsels to try exploring what exactly the other perspective means to the person or group who holds it. Day's guidance: Be an amateur anthropologist, dare to ask "why," and explore a different world from a neutral place.[10] There will be plenty of time to come to your personal evaluation, she counsels, and it will be a more informed stance. Remember how Jesus taught, "Do not judge, so that you may not be judged" (Matthew 7:1).

Eight years ago, a group of laity at Killearn United Methodist Church in Tallahassee, Florida, launched an experiment in difficult conversations with a theology and science group. Wanting to transcend the "growing perception in our society that one must either believe science or religion," participants engaged in informed dialogue. They later reported life-changing experiences, often unexpected, as they discovered how, in God's grace, "science and theology dovetail" in profound ways.[11]

In the wake of tragedy, community conversation is especially difficult, but it also can offer great promise for transformation. In 2007, eight people were killed in a shooting at a shopping center in suburban Omaha, Nebraska, leaving the community deeply shaken. The interfaith coalition Omaha Together One Community organized conversations to discuss gun violence, and they were often uncomfortable. Racial minority representatives asked: where was your concern for gun violence before it hit the suburbs? Subsequent community meetings, eventually involving more than 500 people, allowed for the expression of long-held resentments, the airing of facts, and the "exposure of institutional racism."[12]

Eventually, participants came together to advocate for an expansion of the city's summer youth recreation program. At one signal moment, almost one hundred people descended on the city council chambers: they wore bright yellow stickers reading, "Yes to Youth." The program expansion was approved.

INSTITUTIONAL TRANSFORMATION AND COMMUNITY IMPACT

Institutional change took place in our parable when the ambulance service was started, and more importantly, when the village government took steps to rebuild the road. Institutional transformation happens when basic practices change, when "this is how we have always done it" becomes "we're going to try a new way."

Institutional change can start small, but nevertheless significantly, as when our churches stop using coffee cups made of Styrofoam, which doesn't biodegrade, or begin serving fair-trade coffee, which ensures that small-scale growers and harvesters receive a more equitable share of the profits. Having fruit and vegetables at church coffee hour, for example, shows concern for those who want to eat healthier or are struggling with dietary issues and ailments like diabetes.

On a larger scale, the United Methodist Church of St. Paul and St. Andrew in New York City is engaged in groundbreaking institutional change with its interfaith feeding program. An initiative that provided food for a million meals in 2011, the West Side Campaign Against Hunger demonstrates how a standard church food pantry idea has been reimagined in a transformational way.[13] The program, led by executive director Doreen Wahl, treats its clients as customers and offers them, within various categories, personal choices in the groceries that are distributed.

At each visit, clients check in with a social worker and report on their progress in challenges they face, such as securing food stamps or resolving immigration problems. Social service agencies, eager to bring their assistance into the community, are on hand certain days to provide legal assistance, HIV/AIDS testing, tax return help, and nutrition education. Clients and former clients help staff the food pantry program, and certain unemployed clients receive professional job training as chefs in the kitchen that prepares free daily meals. With its client-empowerment practices, the program has become nationally recognized as a model, helping to influence food pantries and outreach programs across the church and nation.

WORKING FOR SYSTEMIC CHANGE

Most issues ultimately require broad systemic change. This means getting at the root causes. It means fulfilling our baptismal calling "to resist evil, injustice, and oppression."[14] In his day, Wesley fought particularly against poverty, war, smuggling, and slavery. Out of his concern for the poor, he railed against widespread smuggling—the form of tax evasion of his day—because it was a way the rich shifted more of the burden of government funding onto the poor. He vehemently denounced the systemic evil of the slave trade, reserving some of his harshest words to condemn American slavery as "the vilest that ever saw the sun."[15] He vigorously supported William Wilberforce, the Parliament leader, in the fight to abolish the slave trade in the British Empire.

The United Methodist Church, long committed to systemic change, has recently identified ministry with the poor as a special emphasis. The roots of poverty are complex and interconnected. They may include insufficient living wage jobs—inadequate education and health care, illness and disability, and family dysfunction. Over the years, hands-on mission experience has taught that the antidotes to poverty are just as complex and interconnected—a principle that is reflected in the work of such initiatives as the Comprehensive Rural Health Project (CRHP). The India-based program was founded in 1970 by Raj and Mabelle Arole, husband-and-wife physicians committed to serving the rural poor. It has come to encompass every aspect of community health, from nutrition and hygiene to education and income generation.

Perhaps most importantly, through training and assistance, it empowers the villages to sustain the program themselves. The United Methodist General Board of Global Ministries has joined with CRHP to replicate its pioneering work worldwide by bringing volunteers from countries in Africa, Asia, and Latin America to the Jamkhed, India, headquarters for training. Program models have since been launched in Brazil, Zimbabwe, Sierra Leone, Kenya, and the Philippines. This is sacramental living on a global scale.

Walking justly in the governance of their state, Virginia United Methodists have maintained a twenty-year tradition of an annual United Methodist Day at the state's General Assembly. In 2012, 330 United Methodists, most wearing the red and black colors of the denominational cross and flame, flooded the Virginia Capitol and the General Assembly building in Richmond to meet with their representatives on various issues. Patsy Gochenour of Winchester, Virginia, was among them, working to keep the ban on uranium mining in the state intact. Layman Dan Nichols of Richmond came to make sure "the point of view of the lobbyists" isn't all that elected officials hear. Twenty-five members of the Rising Hope United Methodist Mission Church in Alexandria, mostly low-income people, came to let legislators hear, as their pastor Keary Kincannon put it, "from the voices of some of the least among us . . . homeless, disabled, unemployed and working poor, or on fixed incomes. We were asking our legislators not to forget about us."[16]

The 2011 controversy in Wisconsin over legislation to strip bargaining rights from public workers aroused fervent advocacy for the economic justice that Methodists have championed as far back as the original Social Creed of 1908. In a much-quoted letter to Gov. Scott Walker, Wisconsin Bishop Linda Lee cited the *Social Principles of The United Methodist Church*:

> We support the right of all public and private employees to organize for collective bargaining into unions and other groups of their own choosing. Further, we support the right of both parties to protection in so doing and their responsibility to bargain in good faith within the framework of the public interest. . . . [17]

Bishop Lee protested that the governor's initiative "would end the possibility for those who are government employees here in Wisconsin to negotiate settlement of labor and management disagreements." More than 120 religious leaders marched together in a rally of 100,000 protesters.

United Methodist clergywoman C. J. Hawking of Oak Park, Illinois, traveled to be a part of the protest, and reported in **response** magazine that "people returned each day because this marked an extraordinary, transcendent experience of an intimate community. . . . [The state capitol] is the people's cathedral. . . . God's presence is palpable and unmatched in any sustained experience I have ever had in my life." In a remarkable testimony to the real presence of God in the struggle for human dignity, United Methodist pastor Amanda Stein of Madison celebrated an open Communion service in the center of the Capitol rotunda.[18]

PERSONAL LIFESTYLE

Our discussion of the sacraments stressed how sharing in them means taking the reality of Christ into our very selves. To be a part of God's kin-dom movement means allowing our minds and hearts to be remolded. Paul admonished, "Let the same mind be in you that was in Christ Jesus" (Philippians 2:5). When we have "the mind of Christ," our personal lifestyle is one of discipleship and of the social holiness that Wesley advocated. Foundational for our works of mercy, then, is a life that embodies the love and justice we seek. It is about being the change we want to see.

The qualities of social holiness include generosity of time, energy, and money. They include paying attention to others, to the world community, and to our own best intuitions and God's cues as they come to us.

Embracing social holiness means growing into the habits of sacramental living: radical hospitality, the hospitality of Jesus, becomes part of us. We root out jealousy and judgment. Others' pain seems as important as our own. We become more confident in our own capacity to bring change and to be changed. And we seek to align this capacity with God's work in all creation, discovering, with God's help, the moral authority to make a difference for the good.

I HAVE HEARD YOU CALLING IN THE NIGHT

God calls each of us to join the healing stream of God's love and justice, and our baptism is the symbol of that call. But how exactly does God call? Let's consider ways that God shares this yearning for our attention.

The Bible has a wealth of stories about it. Some of the best-known stories depict a clear, even dramatic, call. Sometimes in scripture, God calls faithful persons by name, often repeating the name twice to get attention, as when God called "Moses, Moses" (Exodus 3:4), "Samuel, Samuel" (1 Samuel 3:10), and Jesus called "Martha, Martha" (Luke 10:41), "Saul, Saul" (Acts 9:4).

A beloved hymn in *The United Methodist Hymnal* expresses God's call and our response:

> Here I am, Lord. Is it I, Lord? I have heard you calling in the night.
> I will go, Lord, if you lead me. I will hold your people in my heart.[19]

The story of God's call to the boy Samuel has been a great source of inspiration through the ages. In a time when "the word of the Lord was rare and there were no visions," Samuel, the boy assisting Eli in the temple, hears a voice in the middle of the night. At first, he thinks it's Eli calling and goes running to him. The second time, wise old Eli tells Samuel that it's the Lord calling, and that the next time he should answer God. When he hears, "Samuel, Samuel," the third time in the dead of night, he utters the response that rings down through the ages: "Speak, for your servant is listening." The Lord responds that Samuel is a part of God's plan, and the boy grows up to become a wise and transformative prophet of the Israelites (1 Samuel 3:1–21).

Where do you find yourself in this story? As the one hearing a perplexing voice in the night? As a sage counseling a younger person in the ways of the Lord? Or as one answering to your name being called and responding, "Here I am," beginning a lifetime of doing God's work and leading God's people?

The biblical accounts of God's call are perhaps the most familiar, but God has never stopped finding unlikely times and places to call us by name.

Such was the case one night in 1955, when the Rev. Dr. Martin Luther King Jr. weighed his role in a planned boycott of the Montgomery, Alabama, bus system. Days before, Rosa Parks, a black seamstress and local civil rights leader, had refused to give up her seat at the front of a bus, thus challenging one of the city's many demeaning laws of racial segregation. Professor Jo Ann Robinson and the Women's Political Council took the lead in planning the boycott, and King, an eloquent young pastor who was new in town, was asked to be a spokesman for the quickly accelerating movement.[20]

Already the target of death threats, he answered the phone late one night as his wife and children slept. An anonymous caller spat out the words: "We gonna blow your brains out and blow up your house." Deeply shaken, King put his head in his hands on the kitchen table and told God that he was scared to death and didn't think he had the strength or courage to lead. He then heard an inner voice, the voice of Jesus calling him by name, "Martin Luther, stand up for righteousness. Stand up for justice. . . . I will be with you." King's trembling stopped as he surrendered his will to God's. He experienced an inner peace he'd never felt before. With confidence in a personal God who would never leave him, he accepted an increasingly prominent role in the historic freedom struggle that inspires to this day.[21]

God's call comes in so many ways, and hymns often give them expression, such as this poignant one:

> Softly and tenderly Jesus is calling, calling for you and for me . . .
> Come home, come home . . . [22]

Another hymn, "The Voice of God is Calling," expresses how heavily human pain weighs on God—as it did when God answered Moses in the burning bush, "I have observed the misery of my people" (Exodus 3:7–10):

I hear my people crying in slum and mine and mill;
no field or mart is silent, no city street is still.
I see my people falling in darkness and despair.
Whom shall I send to shatter the fetters which they bear?[23]

God's call may come out of our vulnerability, weakness, or despair: Paul declared from his own intense experience that God's "power is made perfect in weakness" (2 Corinthians 12:9). One hymn writer puts it this way:

Our strength is dust and ashes, our years a passing hour;
But you can use our weakness to magnify your power.[24]

Our friend Maggie Liechty, of Berne, Indiana, received such a call in the crucible of her own great weakness and suffering. An energetic lover of life, she was suddenly stricken with debilitating sensitivities and allergies, a condition known as multichemical sensitivity or environmental illness. Once released from the hospital, she found herself extremely sensitive to scents, airborne chemicals like fertilizer, cleaning products, pollens, dust, and myriad things in the atmosphere that most people hardly notice. Consequently, for some thirty years now, she has had to stay indoors, cloistered in a couple of rooms that have been cleansed of every possible threat. To venture outside leaves her with intensified emotional and physical side effects that can last for days.

What is amazing, though, is that despite all her limitations, near-constant pain, and chronic insomnia, she has carried on a ministry of spiritual companionship with scores of people, whether a college president or recent immigrant. God has claimed her for a new kind of identity and calling and endowed her with resilience, deep gratitude, and infectious joy. Through telephone calls, e-mail, letters, personal visits, and intercession she has been a tower of hope, peace, and strength for many.

While God's calls can come in a single crystallizing moment, perhaps most commonly, they come more or less as a continuous summons, reconfirmed in life's events and marked by pivotal moments.

The life of Methodist Thelma Stevens (1902–1990) reflects an over-arching call resounding over time and punctuated by significant events and changes. Growing up Anglo in rural Mississippi, Stevens played with both African-American and white children. But when school was in session, she was unsettled that her black playmates were not allowed to attend hers, nor were there any schools for them. Still, she couldn't get any of the adults around her to acknowledge or even talk about this gross racial disparity. Then, as a nineteen-year-old teaching in a one-room high school for whites, Stevens was unwittingly coaxed by a group of her students to a wrenching site: a remote clearing in the woods where a crowd had gathered and a black youth was hanging from a tree, the victim of a lynch mob. Devastated by what she had witnessed, she decided that God had brought her to this modern crucifixion, and she vowed that, "if the Lord would ever let me live long enough I would spend the rest of my life working for basic fairness and justice and safety for black people."[25]

The growth of Stevens' calling to serve racial justice continued consistently from one experience to another: violating college rules to arrange contacts with African Americans; cross-racial mentoring of teachers who themselves had only a fifth-grade education; and eventually serving and empowering the black community in Augusta, Georgia, as director of the Bethlehem Center. In 1940 she was recruited to be the executive in Christian social relations for Methodist women's work, and she went on to organize Methodist women to fight for racial justice in myriad ways. Perhaps most significantly, Stevens helped to publish a guide on state segregation laws that aided attorneys fighting to repeal legal segregation; she also helped write the Women's Division's original Charter on Racial Policies. [26]

But now, in this present moment, how do we know when it's "the voice of God" calling *us*? There are many voices vying for our attention. How do we sort them out? This is a matter of Christian discernment, to which we now turn.

CHRISTIAN DISCERNMENT: THE FOUNDATION OF LIVING SACRAMENTALLY[27]

Through Christian discernment, we are given a doorway into God's will and wisdom for each of our lives. We can develop an ability to perceive God's individual and continuing invitation to grow. We can learn how our loving God sees us, in contrast to how we see ourselves. We can begin to glimpse how God is shaping and healing us throughout our lives, in matters large and small.

Christian discernment rests on the assumption that God wants to communicate with us, has a plan for us, and claims and empowers us for living sacramentally and walking justly. Through discernment, we can begin to sense how, even in our seemingly inconsequential lives, God is still making all things new. We can catch glimpses of God's greatness, as God reveals God's self to us. God is still saying today what God said in the prophet Jeremiah's letter to the Hebrew exiles in Babylon:

> For surely I know the plans I have for you, says the Lord, plans for your welfare and not for harm, to give you a future with hope. Then when you call upon me and come and pray to me, I will hear you. When you search for me, you will find me; if you seek me with your heart. (Jeremiah 29:11–13)

Openness to God's prompting on a daily—even hourly—basis can lead to a lively ongoing conversation with God. Discernment can enable us to order our lives in accordance with God's invitation to live sacramentally.

HOW CAN WE HEAR GOD?

Actually, asking how to "hear" God is not the right question for most of us. Sometimes God does indeed seem to speak words that are "heard" in our mind's ear. But God may also communicate through images that are "seen" in our mind's eye. Some people have an exquisite sixth sense of God's nearness and nudging. And to a few, God seems to communicate concepts that reframe old ways of thinking. Often these avenues of communication are combined in surprising ways that leave us saying, "I could not have made that up!" Or maybe, "This sounds a little strange, so I'll discern some more."

One thing is certain: God does not fit into categories or expectations. God does communicate as God chooses: when, where, and how. But you can trust that God knows well the unique pathway to your individual soul and will somehow speak your language.

So, the first step in discernment is asking God to bring forward what God wants you to know. As best as you can, surrender your capacity for human intuition to God's control—and you may have more intuitive capabilities than you realize. Ask the Holy Spirit to shape and control your perceptions and to speak through your hunches, intuition, observations, and expertise. In faith, ask for discernment, then trust that somehow God will give you the sense, image, words, memory, or whatever else is needed for helping, healing, or growth.

Then, pay attention! Open up every capacity you have for awareness; in fact, discerning your call is rooted in noticing. This is true whether you are discerning the direction of your life or just what to do today. Be aware of your emotions, thoughts, and physical self. What images, music, or other sounds play in your mind? What captures your attention as you look at your surroundings or catch up on the news? Continue to ask God to help you understand and respond to these awarenesses.

Keep paying attention as you go about your life. What gives you energy? What human suffering or need ignites special compassion and commitment in you? What suffering of your own gives you wisdom? What excites you? What do you desire most in your deepest self? You might discover how the desires of your heart coincide with the needs of the world.

As you allow an idea of what God wants to take shape, continue to ask God to correct your impressions or strengthen what you have gotten right. You may feel nudged to talk to a particular person, read a particular book, or attend a certain event. Keep paying attention; discover what new awareness will come.

Check your discernment with a mentor or spiritual friend. Such a helper can be a sounding board, tell you whether you are getting off center, or add to your store of knowledge. Quite likely God will speak to you through that helper.

Discernment doesn't always come easily. We cannot compel God, and sometimes we might be too tangled up to perceive anything but our own tiresome inner tapes. Distraction, confusion, or a lot of nothing can greet us as we wait for an answer. When this happens we may need to be patient and try again, asking God to cut through our underbrush as we pray.

Learning to discern God's intention for us can be a wonderfully rich, lifelong journey. Those with years of experience in committed discernment describe how their perceptions seem to sharpen over time, especially as they increasingly trust what they are receiving. For them, the process of discernment seems to happen faster and with less fuss.

However—and this is a big "however"—we need to remember that our discernment can be off. We can be blind and deaf, or just plain wrong, even with the help of friends and mentors. Our own needs, pains, experiences, embarrassments, and viewpoints can distort or drown out God's voice. We can wish for something so hard that we imagine that God wants it, too. We always need to be open to having our discernment change or develop as we live it.

TESTING YOUR DISCERNMENT FOR LIVING SACRAMENTALLY

The more we trust what we receive, the more we take it seriously enough to test it. What might it look like to test discernment? Simply writing down what we think God is communicating can be a small but important act of trust. In crucial matters, however, we should not impulsively leap to action on the basis of one discernment experience; surely we should pray about it further, and let a conviction grow over time. We can continue to mull things over with a friend or spiritual companion. We can let our discernment rest for a while to see whether it is confirmed from other sources. We might try following our discernment provisionally and see what happens. And we might ponder some evaluating questions:

- Could my own need for healing be getting in the way of clarity and effectiveness? Many a social movement has been harmed by participants using it for personal ends or gratification.

- Does my discernment square with the God of the Bible? Is it being true to Christ's spirit? In Wesley's terms, is it in keeping with "the whole scope and tenor" of scripture?

- Does my discernment have the ring of common sense? If not, it would be good to carefully look for confirmation from other sources.

- Is my sense of call consistent with the best human wisdom? Have I bothered to inform myself adequately?

- Does my call fit in with the thinking of the church over time? With the Wesleyan tradition? With the mission and teaching of Jesus (as in Luke 4:18–19)? With the spirit, if not the letter, of *The Social Principles of The United Methodist Church*? (At the same time, we cannot deny that God is still speaking and could be leading the church in a new way.)

- Is my call consistent with special concern for people who are marginalized, poor, and victimized?

- Do those whom I trust the most find my call plausible and consistent with how they see God at work in my life?

- Does my sense of call grow stronger over time or does it go hot and cold? Does it receive confirmation from many directions?

- Is there an element of surprise? Although surprise is not always present, it can point to a genuine call.

- Does my sense of call possibly make me look good or feather my own nest? If so, it's important to be doubly cautious.

- Am I putting up roadblocks to real discernment? For example, am I already certain of what God wants even before I ask? Is part of me unwilling to receive God's attention? Is some sense of shame inhibiting me? Am I stuck, waiting for the *perfect* call or discernment?

- Am I physically able to follow a certain calling? Can I follow this call and also care for my health?

- Am I in danger of taking on more than I can handle? Am I pridefully assuming that my energy is limitless and everything depends on me? How do my family and immediate community accompany me in this discernment process?

- Does my sense of call represent a real challenge? Does it excite me and give me a sense of peace in following it? Or am I doing it out of guilt or some inner or outer compulsion?

- Does my sense of call embrace the practice of the means of grace in word and sacrament, so that I can continually feed on Christ's real presence?

- Does my sense of call make me want to become better prepared to do and be what's necessary?

This is a daunting list of questions. Admittedly, Wesley was much more economical. He asked only four masterfully succinct ones: Does my discernment square with scripture? With tradition? With reason? With experience?

We like to think that our questions simply elaborate on Wesley's Quadrilateral. If you re-read our questions, you might agree that each can be sorted into one of Wesley's categories. We share them with you because they have helped us examine our motives more honestly and have shone a light on God's continuing invitation.

Remember that even with your best efforts and your personal inventories, your discernment may well still be a bit murky with unanswered questions. Discernment is seldom crystal clear. Still, the gospel is full of admonition to go out in strength and to trust God to guide you, empower you, and if necessary, redirect your course.

The following chapter will introduce you to several Christians who have discerned God's call on their lives to live sacramentally and walk justly. As you experience their stories and insights, we invite you to be inspired—and to listen for God's voice speaking through them to you.

1   "A Service of Word and Table," *The United Methodist Hymnal* (Nashville, The United Methodist Publishing House, 1993), 10.

2   Charles Yrigoyen, Jr., *John Wesley: Holiness of Heart and Life* (Nashville: Abingdon Press, 1996), with study guide by Ruth A. Daugherty, 57.

3   From John Wesley's sermon, "Upon Our Lord's Sermon on the Mount, VI," 1748, quoted in Yrigoyen, *John Wesley: Holiness of Heart and Life,* 57–58.

4   The categories of Direct, One-to-One Aid; Education, Conversation, Motivation; Institutional Transformation; and Working for Systemic Change are adapted from a United Methodist Women's analysis shared by a United Methodist Women staff member at the National Office, Carol Barton.

5   Jessica Connor, "Wrapped in Prayer: Quilts Comfort Those in Need," *United Methodist Reporter,* January 5, 2010, 4B.

6   Kathy Gilbert, "From Poverty to Family: Program Makes Room at Table for the Poor," *United Methodist Reporter,* January 13, 2012, 1Aff.

7   Ibid., 4A.

8   "Intercept the Traffickers 2012," *United Methodist Women Action Alert,* December 5, 2011, http://new.gbgm-umc.org/umw/act/alerts/item/index.cfm?id=722.

9   See Katie Day, *Difficult Conversations: Taking Risks, Acting with Integrity* (The Alban Institute, 2001).

10 Ibid., 87–88.

11 Alan Moreton, "Church's Small Group Dedicated to Study of Science and Theology," *United Methodist Reporter,* January 6, 2012, 2B.

12 Donald Bredthauer, "Community Organizing for a Just Response to Violence," William K. McElvaney, *Becoming a Justice Seeking Congregation: Responding to God's Justice Initiative"* (New York, Bloomington: iUniverse, Inc., 2009), 81–88.

13 West Side Campaign Against Hunger, 2011 Annual Report, www.wscah.org.

14 "The Baptismal Covenant IV," *The United Methodist Hymnal* (Nashville, The United Methodist Publishing House, 1993), 50.

15 From Wesley's letter to William Wilberforce, February 24, 1791.

16 Neill Caldwell and Linda Rhodes, "Black and Red All Over: Virginia United Methodist Day at the General Assembly," *Faith in Action,* February 13, 2012, http://www.umc-gbcs.org/site/apps/nlnet/content.aspx?c=frLJK2PKLqF&b=798 1347&ct=11627327.

17 *The Book of Discipline of The United Methodist Church 2008* (Nashville: Abingdon Press, 2008), ¶163B.

18 C. J. Hawking, "A People's Cathedral in Wisconsin," **response**, April, 2011, 35–37.

19 "Here I Am, Lord," *United Methodist Hymnal,* 593.

20 Lynne Olson, *Freedom's Daughters: The Unsung Heroines of the Civil Rights Movement from 1830 to 1970* (New York: Scribner, 2001), 87–99.

21 Stephen B. Oates, *Let the Trumpet Sound: The Life of Martin Luther King, Jr.* (New York: Harper and Row, Publishers, 1982), 88–89.

22 "Softly and Tenderly Jesus is Calling," *United Methodist Hymnal,* 348.

23 "The Voice of God Is Calling," *United Methodist Hymnal,* 436.

24 Ibid.

25 Alice G. Knotts, "Thelma Stevens, Crusader for Racial Justice," in Rosemary Skinner Keller, *Spirituality and Social Ministry: Vocational Vision of Women in the United Methodist Tradition* (Nashville: Abingdon Press, 1993), 232.

26 Ibid., 234–37.

27 Much of the following is adapted or quoted from Tilda Norberg, *Consenting to Grace: An Introduction to Gestalt Pastoral Care* (New York: Penn House Press, 2006), 88–98.

a regular time period to review the Life discipline, such as on my birthday, etc)

_____

What do I need to do to make time for these practices?

Daily:_____

Weekly:_____

Monthly:_____

Annually:_____

Additional notes below and on the back:

_____

_____

_____

_____

Worksheet for Creating a Life Discipline

My Practices (eg. Scripture reading, spiritual reading, centering prayer, Christian conferencing, Holy Communion, fasting, seeing a spiritual director, worship, works of mercy, etc)

I commit to the following practices:

Daily: _____

Weekly: _____

Monthly: _____

Annually: _____

Works of Mercy Works of mercy are the result of our connecting more and more with God through works of piety and they are also spiritual practice, facilitating our connection with God.

I commit to the following works of mercy: _____

What needs to change in my schedule to make room for Life Discipline practices I am committing to?

_____

_____

What additions and planning steps do I need to make? (eg. scheduling of annual retreat, deciding on

CHAPTER 4

Faith Is a Verb

By Nancy Kruh

The last place Bette Buschow wanted to be was in prison. But on this fine spring day in 2003, that's exactly where she was heading.

The friends she'd been visiting in Austin, Texas, were volunteers in a prison ministry at a nearby women's facility, and they had invited her to the program's "graduation."

"They said, 'Come, go with us—you'll like it,' " recalls Buschow, who lives in Bedford, Texas, a middle-class suburb between Dallas and Fort Worth.[1]

Prison? Like it? An image immediately sprang to her mind. Cinderblock walls, iron bars, barbed wire. A place for society's rejects. "I figured they were in prison because they deserved to be, and I didn't want to think about them."

When Buschow got in the car with her friends that morning for the day's activities, she had planned to be dropped off to visit a family member in the afternoon while the couple went on to the prison. But time ran short. Any detour and the graduation would be missed. And that's how Buschow found herself behind those cinderblock walls, sitting in a gymnasium with a group of inmates, listening to the program graduates' life stories.

"About halfway through, I started crying," she recalls. "It touched my heart so much, and it was so unexpected. The women were telling their stories, but it was so much like my upbringing. I grew up right next to the railroad tracks. It may have been on the right side, but we were poor. I knew what it was like to be poor and what it was like to be lonely. Thinking back, I was probably in an emotionally abusive situation with my mother. I only got to college because I earned scholarships. That kind of social and economic marginalization—I had experienced enough of that. These women and I, we were much more alike than different."

Though Buschow didn't realize it at the time, reflecting now on the experience, she knows she had been perfectly primed to hear God's call at that moment. She was just finishing a master's degree in theology at Brite Divinity School at Texas Christian University, and she was trying to decide whether to pursue a doctorate. A physician's wife, mother of two, and a member of a United Methodist fellowship, she had returned to school as her nest emptied to "develop my mind in a way I hadn't before and to develop spiritually in a way I hadn't before." But as much as she was enjoying this later-life education, a new realization was giving her pause: "Does it really matter how many angels can dance on the head of a pin, and isn't it time to live this instead of think about it?"

After the prison ministry's graduation ceremony, the inmates gathered around Buschow. They had seen her tears and came to comfort her. It was, she says, "instant rapport." Before that moment, she says, she had always believed "that God is incarnate in all of us." At the same time, she also understood it's easy to look at the "other" and "not recognize them as a child of God." As the inmates reached out to her, Buschow found herself "in the right frame of mind to recognize it deeply. Experiencing the interaction with these women just verified it."

What had never even been on her radar quickly became Buschow's all-consuming passion. Soon she was driving to Lockhart almost weekly with a growing group of friends in tow to participate in the prison ministry. Then, in 2005, she launched her own initiative closer to home, serving the women's jailhouse population in Dallas County. Called *Resolana*, a

Spanish word for a warm, protected place to gather, the program today has oversight of a sixty-four-bed "tank" in the jail, where an army of volunteers offers support and instruction in the areas of mental health, life skills, creativity, wellness, and twelve-step recovery.

In her work, the sixty-three-year-old Buschow has discovered that "faith is a verb. . .Where Jesus interacted and where his ministry took him, I get it." But Resolana doesn't proselytize. Instead, it meets participants spiritually "wherever they are on their faith journey," she explains. "I have very strong feelings that you don't impose a faith on someone that way. But what we do is totally faith-based in a different sense. What we're doing is all about holy ground. What we're about is redeeming people in a very non-restrictive use of that term. It's all about faith. We don't label them religiously, but what we're doing is hugely spiritual."

These days, Buschow often hears the question, asked with a mixture of astonishment and incredulity: "How can you do what you do?" Often, it's asked by the sort of person she was just a few short years ago. Her answer: "How can you not?"

OUTSIDE YOUR COMFORT ZONE

It may surprise. It may shout. It may whisper. It may swell slowly over time. God's call settles differently on each listener. And when it does, we can expect it to unsettle. Truly, if this is the voice of God—the creator of all things, the giver of every breath we take—then how can we not respond?

In the previous chapter, we learned about ways to discern God's call. It can be a challenge. We may not know how to respond at first. But that doesn't necessarily mean we have to wait for perfect clarity. "My advice is, start moving," says Dave Knapp, an Ohio car dealer with a passion for disaster-relief mission work. "Understand that life is about serving others, then you're going to find your calling."[2]

Raised a Catholic, Knapp strayed from church in adulthood before returning in 2002 to Ginghamsburg United Methodist Church, a large, mission-oriented congregation in Tipp City, Ohio. In those first few Sundays in the pew, he began to feel a nudge he sensed was coming from God. The church urges its members into a daily habit of Bible study, and as Knapp plunged into scripture, "I started to feel the Holy Spirit move in me." Over time, he jettisoned friendships he came to consider unhealthy; he grew more patient and forgiving in the relationships that mattered. He made donations to help youth mission trips, and he supported other church ministries. His car dealership launched an annual cancer charity run. "I've had what the Bible would call a cheerful giver's heart," he says. Yet for all the good works, the nudge continued insistently.

He listened as his pastor stressed the importance of service, and particularly "to serve outside your comfort zone." He preached: "Meet the people right where they are, right in their need."

In September 2005, Knapp joined the rest of the nation in watching news coverage of Hurricane Katrina's destruction of New Orleans and the Gulf Coast. "My heart was just poured out," he recalls, "but I didn't move right away. It was kind of weird. I heard so much and didn't process any of it."

But three months later, Knapp ran into a neighbor who was outfitting two work trailers and headed to Slidell, Louisiana, a hard-hit town north of New Orleans. A simple invitation to join the small work team finally set Knapp in motion. It was time to leave his "comfort zone."

Once amid the devastation, though, he was startled to discover, "I wasn't outside my comfort zone at all. God had prepared me for the mission field my whole life." Knapp's father was a contractor who made sure his son was handy with every kind of tool. Knapp's love for cooking kept the team well fed. In the many church-sponsored trips that have since followed, Knapp also has put his formidable leadership skills to work.

Over the years, he has built relationships with the people he's helped that "I'll cherish my whole life. I've met so many people, and I've become a blessing to many of them and they've become a blessing to me." He also has experienced a "great transformation" in the bonds he has forged with other work team members. "Church is outside the four walls," Knapp says. "That's where faith becomes action. Being in a small group—to be accountable to others and for others to be accountable to you—that's called holiness."

After a dozen trips to Louisiana, Iowa, and Haiti, the sixty-one-year-old Knapp has never stopped feeling the nudge, and he revels in responding to it. "I'm led and compelled to do the great commission that Jesus has called us to do," he explains. "I've got this conviction in my heart to leave this world totally exhausted to do his will for what he has done for me and in me."

A PERSISTENT CALL

In Knapp's case, God's persistence took the form of a spiritual push to get moving. For Jenni Yeoh, it took a much more human form. While the Tacoma, Washington, resident was attending a United Methodist Women event in San Francisco several years ago, she decided to visit Gum Moon Women's Residence and Asian Women's Resource Center, a United Methodist mission in Chinatown. "I am Chinese, and I wanted to see what they offered in the Chinese culture," explains Yeoh, a longtime United Methodist Women leader. She hit it off with executive director Gloria Tan, who invited her to return and volunteer with the residents. The mission, which serves low-income women in dire circumstances, impressed Yeoh. Perhaps, she thought, she would take Tan up on the invitation. . .someday.[3]

Another trip to San Francisco offered the opportunity for lunch with Tan, and the invitation was again extended. Again, Yeoh deferred. Tan persisted. She "kept calling me to come," Yeoh says. "She'd say, 'Are you coming this year?' And the next year, she asked again."

Finally, Yeoh realized it was time. Traveling alone, she spent several days with the women. Fluent in five languages, she was able to hear their stories and lead a workshop on jewelry making. "They gave me a chance to be their friend," Yeoh says. "I am blessed by them more than them by me. Their strength inspires me. They live with very little, but the fact they were able to survive whatever they survived, that inspires me."

So much so that Yeoh knew she wanted other women from her church to experience the Gum Moon residents. Since that first visit, she has led groups to the San Francisco mission seven times to get acquainted with the residents and conduct craft workshops. "The reason I bring the women is because I see the impact it makes on them after the trip, the changes in their thinking and in their lives."

Yeoh's involvement with Gum Moon has become an integral part of her faith journey. "What is God requiring me to do?" she asks, paraphrasing the indelible Micah 6:8 passage that urges believers to "act justly, love kindness, and to walk humbly with your God." Yeoh, sixty-five, reflects: "If I don't do the justice part or the kindness part, then how can I walk humbly with God?"

"EVERYONE SHOULD BE IN MISSION"

No matter how God calls us, we are called to act—not only on God's claim on our lives, but also in faith. We follow, often not understanding where God is leading us, and often discovering we are headed into unexpected territory.

In her youth, Robin Ball served a stint in the Peace Corps in Botswana, then later traveled to Tonga and Zimbabwe to do church mission work. In her early fifties, she and her husband were running a property management company in Pagosa Springs, Colorado, when she heard an undeniable call to become a missionary. "It was during a worship service," recalls Ball, who is a member of Community United Methodist Church.[4] "They were talking about acts of mercy and acts of justice, and all the different ways in the world that they can be done." The service ended with the hymn "The Summons": 'Will you come and follow me if I but call your name? Will you go where you don't know and never be the same?'"[5]

As she sang the words, Ball felt "a warming of the heart, a warming of the spirit, and also just a clarity. It's like, aha! I know what I'm here for and

I know that's what I'm supposed to do." Yet such clarity came with a price. "How does this happen?" she wondered, wrestling with the implications. "I have a family, a business. How can I pick up and go be a missionary? I hear you calling, but what does that mean?"

Her struggle for discernment was in full sway when, out of the blue, she received an invitation to become the assistant dean of Mission u (United Methodist Women's Conference School of Christian Mission). Instead of going out in the field herself, Ball would be teaching others about the church's mission in a global context, as well as guiding them into mission opportunities. She didn't have to think before she said yes. "This," she says, "is what I was meant to do."

The learning curve was steep, Ball recalls, and within a few months it grew even steeper: The school's dean became seriously ill and had to step down. Ball stepped up with trepidation, but soon found herself being led to all the people and information she needed to get the job done.

In three fulfilling years as dean, Ball has become convinced that "this is a basic education that every Methodist should listen to and think about. It does so many wonderful things to develop your own theology. How do you live your Methodism every day? How can each and every one of us be a missionary and what does mission look like? The only missionaries aren't those who give up their lives and move to Africa. I think that's our stereotype."

"What are the needs in your community and the world, and what are your resources, and how do you combine those? That's my mission, because everyone should be in mission."

WORKING FOR GOD

Jeff Murrell grew up with such a swirl of interests that he struggled for years trying to discern how God wanted him to use his gifts. In school, he excelled in the sciences, and he also was fired by his faith. The son of a Montgomery, Alabama, sanitation worker, he was sensitized at an early age to conservation when his father brought home other people's "trash" that still had obvious usefulness.[6]

"When I was growing up, my mom always said, 'The way you study, you're like a little professor,' so I thought I'd be a professor," says the forty-three-year-old Murrell. "Then my brother had a seizure when I was in ninth grade, and I felt so helpless, so I thought I should become a physician. But I went to Vanderbilt and realized I wasn't cut out to be a physician, so I went to my backup, which was engineering."

After his freshman year, Murrell came home to Montgomery to be a summer missionary for his Southern Baptist church, leading backyard Bible studies and vacation Bible school. By the time he turned twenty-one, he felt he was being called to be a deacon, a servant leader's role in the Southern Baptist tradition. His pastor, though, quashed that idea, interpreting 1 Timothy Chapter 3 to mean Murrell first had to be married to qualify.

Stung by the rejection, Murrell drifted from church after he graduated and began to pursue an engineering career, then he found his way to a United Methodist congregation in the mid-1990s after he married. Reenergized, he learned about United Methodism's home missioner program, which provides men with the opportunity to serve in a lifetime lay relationship with the church. Like the deaconess program for women, home missioners identify what they want to do in a "helping profession" or "church-related vocation" to undertake a ministry of love, justice, and service. Becky Louter, the executive secretary of the Office of Deaconess and Home Missioner Program, told Murrell how John Wesley considered the world his parish. Seized by the idea, Murrell "prayed about it and decided, yep, it's what I want to do."

By the time he was commissioned in 2009, he was working for the U.S. Army Corps of Engineers in munitions—not exactly a field rife with opportunities for a ministry of love, justice, and service. But Murrell stayed faithful in prayer and discernment, and one day, he had a vision that he was about to have a life-changing encounter. Later that same day, a coworker invited him to become part of a new Corps of Engineers environmental program. The goal was to reduce energy costs and consumption at the Department of Defense, the largest single energy consumer in the country.

Suddenly, everything came together for Murrell—his engineering skills, his faith, and his reverence for the earth's resources. This new role would allow him to spread the gospel of environmental stewardship. Today, he travels the world, monitoring energy consumption and creating strategies to control and reduce energy dependence. Still based in Montgomery, he also takes his conservation message out to United Methodist Women groups on a volunteer basis.

"This world belongs to God, and we're just passing through," Murrell says. "What we do is a determination of how we take the blessings God gave us and give back." Now, when he goes to work, "I don't work for me. The bottom line is, I work for God. I work for Jesus. The environment touches all of our lives."

READY TO FOLLOW

Just as discernment can take time—and detours—it also can encounter external obstacles, as Murrell unhappily discovered. While attending a Bible college, Debbie Humphrey experienced a similar blow when her profound call to ministry was invalidated.[7]

"I loved getting up and speaking about God," the fifty-four-year-old Cookson, Oklahoma, woman recalls. "I knew I had to go deeper into it. It was a feeling to the bone. I went to my counselor and I told him I wanted to become a minister, and he said, 'You may be called to be a minister's wife.' I said, 'Oh no, I understand my calling.' And he said, 'No, you don't. Be a teacher, a missionary."

"It was a major letdown, and I thought maybe I didn't understand my calling. But I kept going back to: I know what I know. I know what I feel. It's alive and I can't let it go."

She eventually did marry, and Humphrey and her husband volunteered with their church's youth program. When the couple separated, though, she was asked to step down. Her response was to turn her back on church life. "It kind of left a sour taste in my mouth, and that was bad," she says. "If I was stronger in my faith, I would have continued on. I would not have let anyone stop me to where God was leading me. So I had to grow stronger in my faith, so I could say, 'Okay, God, I'm ready to follow you.'"

It was a lengthy path—through ten years as a city employee in Fort Smith, Arkansas, to a move in 2002 to rural eastern Oklahoma, where Humphrey reconnected with her Choctaw roots and pursued her interest in craft-making. The change of scenery, though, still didn't help her shake off a sense of loneliness and stagnation.

"I needed a [church] family to keep me in check, to assure me, to help me grow," she says. "I knew I had to do something different. I knew God was tugging at my heart."

Intent on finding a new faith home, Humphrey accepted a chance invitation to attend Canterbury Chapel United Methodist Church, where she "really started to get to know about Methodists and Methodism, and I loved their caring and knowledge of people."

Her burgeoning interest drew her to the nearby Cookson Hills Center, a United Methodist Women-sponsored mission that serves the surrounding Cherokee community. There, Humphrey reconnected to her passion for youth work; her time led to a paid staff position as a program coordinator in 2006.

"The youth were the first to help me grow back in the strength," she says. "In teaching them, it helped bring me back to God. When children pray, they pray with their hearts. It brought me back to the God that lives in my heart."

Humphrey works with a population at risk of all the predictable consequences of poverty: broken homes, juvenile delinquency, illiteracy, drug and alcohol abuse, early pregnancy. Clearly, she is undaunted by the challenges, no doubt because she easily sees herself in the young people she serves. Raised in poverty by an abusive, alcoholic father, Humphrey has used her ministry to transform the pain of her own past into an intense empathy.

"I've been there and done that, and I know you can climb out of it," she says. "Even now I'm still climbing out of it."

In 2008, Humphrey received her commission as a United Methodist deaconess to further live out her calling. "I just follow God," she says. "Sometimes I don't know how I do what I do except for the power of God that holds us up. Sometimes I see the children hurting, and it just hurts, but I can't be anywhere else. I don't see myself anywhere else. This is where God led me, and I don't see me doing anything else but serving God."[8]

MINISTERING "AS A WOMAN"

Rosangela Oliveira knows she is fortunate to have come of age in what she calls a "historical moment." In 1975, just four years before she entered a Methodist seminary in her native Brazil, the church there had begun ordaining women, clearing a path for Oliveira and others like her to pursue their call to ministry. Though she was raised in a profoundly patriarchal culture, Oliveira received nothing but encouragement from her parents, whose childhood poverty had deprived them of educational opportunities. But the male-dominated environment at the seminary had yet to fully adjust to the recent change.[9]

"I started to hear that women were here to get married or to learn to be good church secretaries," Oliveira recalls. She fully realized the "implications of discrimination" when professors and other church leaders began to formulate a rule forbidding women clergy from marrying. Soon, Oliveira joined a group of seminary students who organized a response, relying on the writings of Wesley to help make their case. Their well-argued letter persuaded church leaders to back down from the proposal.

Though Oliveira went on in her early twenties to serve three congregations as a pastor, her seminary experience ignited a lifelong passion for advancing the lives of women through the church. What began as a call to ministry had developed into a call to "be in church as a woman and to develop a ministry in the church with women and as a woman." After serving as a women's pastoral advisor on the local level, she advanced to working with women at the district level, then regionally, and finally internationally. From 2001 to 2012, Oliveira served in New York as United Methodist Women's regional missionary to Latin America.

"There is a need to develop ministries so women can have power and voice in their spirituality," explains Oliveira, who, at age fifty-four, assumed the executive directorship of the World Day of Prayer International Committee in 2012. "For me, when you look concretely at church, women are the church; women are the majority in the church. But when you look at churches as structural institutions, you don't get a sense that women are the church. We need to claim our voices in church, then be in ministry to other women. In a sense, my call has been to create the opportunity to strengthen and empower women's response to God in their lives."

Over the years, Oliveira looked upon her role in Latin America as a catalyst: reaching across barriers and borders to draw women out of isolation and bring them together, then connect them to the community organizations that could magnify their power as individuals. In describing her work, Oliveira spurns the word "help."

"'Help' is 'I have it and I'm giving it,'" she says. "I like to use words like 'create opportunity,' or 'mutuality' or even 'friendship.' When you allow one group to be in relationship to another, they become empowered and bring even more into the process."

Oliveira's passion has been fueled by the everyday wisdom she has encountered in her connectional activity. In the "sacred space" of women sharing their experiences with one another, she has felt herself "in the presence of very wise women who are not necessarily educated. The wise woman is one who knows how to deal with life in all kinds of challenges—poverty, violence, health issues. When I can meet those women, I feel very honored and blessed. It inspires me."

"MOTIVATED AND DETERMINED"

When Bethanie Edwards-Goff first heard her call during a sermon on the "joy of giving," she thought of herself as the sort of person who could rarely say no to a sale. "I used to shop all the time," explains the thirty-eight-year-old homemaker and mother of three. "It was mainly clothes. I know I spent more than I should have, just so I could have a new outfit."[10]

As she listened to the sermon, though, she felt something stir. Perhaps it was guilt "for spending so much time on clothing and silly stuff like that." Perhaps it was a realization she had been trying to fill a void. The pastor spoke about how "we're the body of Christ and we are supposed to help one another," and Edwards-Goff unexpectedly found herself taking the words to heart.

She'd heard similar words before, she admits, but "I thought it was about other people's problems, that someone else was supposed to take care of it. Or, if they're that bad off, it's their fault. I didn't have a lot of compassion."

Now, she felt certain, God was calling her to make an about-face. Edwards-Goff reached out for opportunity in the United Methodist Women group in her church, St. Luke's United Methodist Church in Indianapolis, and soon she became known among its membership by an entirely new identity: the sort of person who could rarely say no to a volunteer opportunity.

If it needed doing, Edwards-Goff invariably said yes: organizing the church food drive. Buying gifts for needy families. Running charity sales for a community center and mission work. Editing the United Methodist Women's newsletter. Taking up collections of prenatal vitamins and toys for a hospital in Sierra Leone.

Why yes? "I think I'm motivated and determined to help others in every way that I can, and I try to get other people motivated in the same way," she says. "In the Bible it says to give to the poor without judgment. It shouldn't be who we deem worthy. It should be to anyone and everyone in need."

Edwards-Goff has now set her sights on an international mission trip, hopefully with her family in tow. "I now have something to focus on, to work toward. I like to have a purpose now. And I want my kids to be thinking that way, too."

DOING AN ABOUT-FACE

One of Marcia Bent's favorite Gospel passages tells the story of a woman who "had been suffering from hemorrhages for twelve years." Amid the press of a crowd, she musters the courage to reach out and touch Jesus' garment. Instantly, she is healed. Jesus wheels around and demands she identify herself. When she falls to his feet, he proclaims, "your faith has made you well" (Luke 8:43–48).

"In that culture, she was pretty bold," says Bent.[11] "I'm not particularly bold. Actually, I would say I'm not bold at all." Which is why it's remarkable that this self-described shy New Yorker has found her faith expression in performing publicly. Sometimes, Bent has discovered, God's call includes a personal challenge to act counter to how we may see ourselves.

A native of Jamaica who came to New York City in 1985 in search of work opportunities, Bent found her church home in St. John's United Methodist Church of Elmont, a diverse congregation on Long Island. She quickly became involved in United Methodist Women, in time serving as the group's vice president, then president.

"I see the hand of God working throughout all of that," says the fifty-eight-year-old medical secretary. "Growing up, and even as an adult, . . . I wouldn't really talk much, definitely not in public. The main thing that got that out of me is United Methodist Women."

Attending a United Methodist Women jurisdictional assembly in 2004, Bent saw a woman perform the creation story in the form of biblical storytelling, "and it really impressed me. She told the story and involved the audience, and I just thought that's a good way to tell a Bible story. I thought that's something I'd like to do." It stayed a thought for several months—until Bent learned of a church-sponsored weekend workshop on biblical storytelling.

The workshop was designed to gradually draw participants out of their shells and onto center stage. By the event's end, Bent was ready to try out what she'd learned for a familiar and supportive audience, her United Methodist Women group. As she grew more comfortable with her skills, Bent went to her pastor and asked if she could organize a storytelling group in the congregation.

Another workshop prepared an entire flock of storytellers, and today, about fifteen take turns each week dramatizing the scripture reading during Sunday service. "When we first started, most people in the congregation didn't understand what it was," Bent recalls. "Now they've gotten to the point where they expect it."

Over the years, she has witnessed how storytelling reaches into people's spirits in ways that simple recitation does not. "I really feel it's a powerful tool," she says. "It's a way to break the ice, to tell them about Jesus, to tell them about God." Storytelling also has had a deep impact on Bent's faith and tightened her embrace of scripture. "It puts you into the Spirit. You really have to get that story in you, and the Spirit of God is in you in order to tell the story."

As a result, she says, "I think I'm much more in tune to my spiritual self. I listen to more urgings." She has no doubt those "urgings" emanate from the same source that first brought her to storytelling: "It's the Holy Spirit."

CONSTANT OPPORTUNITIES

God's call can come forcefully, unmistakably, but rarely does it arrive with a step-by-step instruction manual. As much as we may know what God beckons us to do, it's up to us to figure out the way. So it was with Cathy Mejia, who was certain at an early age that God wanted her to engage in some sort of mission work. Growing up in El Salvador, "I was exposed to a lot of missionaries and I really admired them," explains the forty-two-year-old violin teacher. "A lot of people knew I had the call, but they asked me where, and I said, 'I don't know.'"[12]

And so she struck out—to Honduras, Spain, Morocco—but despite the ministry work she accomplished, she knew "this is not it, not yet. When I knew God was calling me, I knew I wouldn't go alone. I was praying, if I was going to get married, my call would be my husband's call, too."

Back in El Salvador, Mejia resumed her music-teaching career, and she became engaged to a pastor. But still, "there was no peace" in her heart. "It's like you're fighting with your own being," she says. "You're thinking and trying to put it together, but it doesn't go together. When I finished that relationship, even though it hurt, there was so much relief. A mountain came off my back. I felt at peace."

Family and church connections finally led Mejia to a most unlikely pairing: a Salvadoran-American bachelor who was a United Methodist pastor in Kentucky. All it took was a bit of matchmaking from the man's uncle, who was the pastor of the church where Mejia was serving as worship leader. Her mother and his mother, as well as church members, offered their own encouragement to Mejia.

"It began with a phone call, and after that, I think AT&T got very rich," she says with a chuckle. When the two finally met, "I felt not only he was the right person, but I also felt like I was being obedient to God."

Yet, the decision to marry and move to Kentucky was wrenching. "It really broke my heart to leave my home, my job, my friends," she says. "But still I knew I was on the right path. There was hardship, but there was also peace. Peace doesn't mean there won't be hardship."

Since coming to Kentucky in 2001, Mejia has become a full partner in her husband's ministry, opening her life to the constant opportunities that God puts in her path. For several years, the couple traveled the state, helping to plant Hispanic congregations.

A United Methodist Women leader recognized Mejia's gifts and invited her to be a language coordinator, even though, at the time, Mejia wasn't sure what United Methodist Women was. "So they shared with me the vision of mission, and I said, 'This is it! My call to mission is going to be fulfilled if I join UMW and I went nuts about it.'" In her new role, Mejia was able to help draw Hispanic women to United Methodist Women, involving them in retreats and Mission u (School of Christian Mission).

In 2009, her husband took a pulpit at Mosaic United Methodist, a church in Louisville that was born out of the merger of five dying congregations. The couple's work to heal the differences, Mejia says, has brought them closer to each other and to God. "We're beginning to see people wanting to connect to mission. The congregation is about 60 percent elderly, so I see people beginning to say, 'I can't go, but I can pay for someone to go.' So you begin to see passion."

Mejia talks excitedly about attracting new members to the church, starting a Bible study, helping an orphanage in El Salvador, and doing mission work in Honduras. Still a violin teacher, she sees spiritual opportunity in getting "the best" from her students because "that's what God wants." Every aspect of her life holds the possibility of responding to God's will—of living sacramentally.

"When people say, 'You have a purpose in life,' I say I feel God has a purpose in my life," Mejia says. "My whole being is living for God. No matter what I am, no matter what I do, it's for God."[13]

A CLEAR PATH TO A CALLING

Brendan Kleiboer entered the University of Michigan intent on being the next Steven Spielberg. But a part-time job at the university's natural history museum caused an abrupt change in focus—and ever since, he's been blessed to see a clear path toward what he's certain is a lifetime calling to pediatric medicine.[14]

"I taught about prehistoric life and ecosystems, and I loved working with kids," the twenty-seven-year-old Grand Rapids, Michigan, man recalls. "I just loved seeing kids have that 'aha!' moment, where you taught them something they didn't know and they got excited about it, and I fed off their enthusiasm. I can't explain it except I just felt a pull. It's kind of an instinctive feeling."

Besides enjoying a special rapport with children, Kleiboer also knows a lifetime spent managing a mild bleeding disorder has given him an unusual empathy for children who are ill.

Raised in the Catholic Church, he also is inspired by two simple but powerful messages he absorbed growing up: God has laid claim to our lives, and God requires us to care for one another. "I think a lot about how I must have gotten this drive and these instincts and these talents and gifts from somewhere, and I'd be wasting them if I didn't use them in the best way possible," Kleiboer says. "I don't think much about, would I be letting God down? It tends to be more personal. I feel I've been given a gift and how can I best use it?"

His favorite Bible passages seem to answer that question. "Whatever you did for the least of my brothers you did for me (Matthew 25:40); blessed are the poor and the meek and the hungry (Matthew 5:3–10)," he says, paraphrasing. "Those things really stick out to me."

With such a confluence of gifts and convictions, his call seems obvious: "I have a particularly big heart for sick kids. It's hard to explain other than, one day, I started to get this nagging feeling that I would be really excited to work with families in a healthcare setting. It's the educational stimulation and the chance to work with people that attract me."

Acceptance into medical school took longer than he anticipated, but Kleiboer didn't fritter away his time as he waited. Instead, he went looking for opportunities to work with children and found Project Transformation (PT), a United Methodist internship program that offers free after-school activities and summer camp for low-income children in the Dallas area. Growing up in a middle-class home and attending private schools, Kleiboer says he "never really thought about poverty much," but that changed in an instant.

"I learned a lot about the families," he says about his two years with PT. "The most significant moments I experienced were when parents would approach me about how their kids were doing in school. Many would say they didn't know what they would do without PT. The thing that stuck out the most was how desperately they wanted a better life for their kids than what they had. I don't know much about where they came from or their citizenship status, but it did seem like almost exclusively the parents really wanted the best for their kids at whatever cost. That was universal."

No doubt his experience with the program continues to influence Kleiboer as he studies at Michigan State University College of Human Medicine. "There are so many opportunities to do community service as a doctor," he says. "For all the kids I'll work with, my goal will be to help them grow up healthy and set up for their best chance to take care of themselves as adults. Education takes as a big a role in that as their physical health."

DOING WHAT COMES NATURALLY

A jolt, a pull, an awakening, a realization: these are typical descriptions of how some people receive their call. But for others, answering God's call can be so natural, even innate, that they may define it simply as the way they go about their lives.

Debby Campbell is surprised that her pastor has even suggested her as someone who is "living out a call." No matter that the sixty-four-year-old retired schoolteacher spends up to seventy hours each week on Get Healthy DeSoto, a community health initiative for her tiny hometown of DeSoto, Missouri. Since she took over the project in 2004—for what was supposed to be a four-month stint—she has occasionally received pay from grants, but most of her work has been voluntary.[15]

Over the years, Campbell has been the catalyst for a wide assortment of health-oriented programs and activities, from organizing exercise classes to establishing walking trails; from rallying the town's restaurants to offer healthier fare to recruiting area farmers to participate in a seasonal market, set up weekly in the parking lot of her church, St. Andrew's United Methodist.

Asked about how she is motivated by her faith, she demurs. It's just not the sort of thing she has the time to think about.

She's pressed: considers the question but thinks the answer is self-evident. "It's just so important," she replies. "I can see a difference in people. I can see that people can change."

She pauses. "Yes," she says, finally and firmly. "I do. I never really thought about it, but that is a true statement. I think God would be terribly disappointed if he gave me all these opportunities and I let them float by and didn't act on them."

And that, she says, is all the understanding she needs. Her community work, she says, "is just who I am. You take what God has given you, and you make the best of it."

"A BIG DIFFERENCE IN SMALL WAYS"

The idea of "answering a call" was so remote to Jessica Johnson when she began her community-organizing work around 2007 that it's taken her almost all of the years since to apply that expression to what she does.[16]

"I have always had a sense that as a part of my spiritual life I ought to be doing something to help others and be active in the world," says the thirty-four-year-old Phoenix attorney. "It wasn't like a lightning bolt struck, or like I was looking and I had to find something. It just came together. The more I got involved, the more I felt that this is the way I should be in the world and that my church should be in the world, working on systemic change and working with families."

Johnson's church, Asbury United Methodist, is among more than thirty-five congregations and community groups involved in the Valley Interfaith Project, a coalition that addresses a comprehensive list of concerns, including education, health care, immigration reform, and transportation.

In a city hard hit by unemployment, Johnson has embraced job creation and training as her personal cause. Most weeks, she spends several hours attending organizational meetings, doing fund-raising, lobbying local leaders, and knocking on doors to spread the word about job training programs.

"I've been at it long enough to see how it's changed me and, in a variety of ways, how it's changed others," Johnson says. "You have to have that dedication to see it through to witness that whole development."

Over time, she has watched as other church members have caught the passion for the work, as once-voiceless community members have become leaders, as young people who have completed job training are now on their way to fulfilling careers. In herself, Johnson has seen a transformation into someone who can "stand up in front of 200 people and say, 'Mr. Mayor, we want you to put money into this very important work.' I feel confident as a person speaking publicly out of my religious beliefs."

Doing this work has given Johnson "a sense that I am who I'm supposed to be, that I'm using the God-given talents I have."

"Obviously one person can't solve all the problems," she adds, "but you can make a big difference in small ways. I've found a lot satisfaction in baby steps toward addressing the bigger problem."

STARTING YOUR OWN ORAL HISTORY PROJECT

Every day, countless United Methodists around the globe are heeding God's call to live sacramentally and walk justly. Stories of such service can function as an inspiration for others, as a validation of the experience, and as important documentation of our collective United Methodist history. But rarely is the time and effort taken to record personal accounts and testimonies of faith.

If you are interested in undertaking an oral history project of the mission work of your church or United Methodist Women group, the following is some guidance to get you started:

■ **Select subjects to interview.** Even if it's a church-wide mission initiative, you don't have to interview everyone to tell a complete story. A few carefully chosen subjects can offer the various points of view you'll need to construct an accurate three-dimensional account.

- **Compose a list of questions.** Think about what you want to ask and write it down. How did your subject hear the call? How did he or she respond? What obstacles were encountered? How did God offer guidance? Avoid "yes" and "no" questions in favor of open-ended queries. You should have enough questions on your list to help keep the interview flowing for at least forty-five minutes to an hour.

- **Be explicit in your invitation.** When you set up an appointment, tell your subject what the time commitment will be and the general discussion topics that will be covered. This will give your subject advance time to prepare, reflect, and remember.

- **Interview your subjects individually.** Resist the temptation to interview your subjects in groups. Individual interviews encourage candor and rapport. Also, subjects who are shy about talking about themselves often feel more comfortable in a one-on-one setting.

- **Record the interview.** Don't rely on taking notes to capture the interview. Today's digital recorders are small, relatively inexpensive, and easy to use. Recordings also are easy to store on computers or disks. Just make sure you keep fresh batteries on hand when you conduct the interview!

- **Be an attentive listener.** Don't interrupt or suggest a word or phrase your subject may be searching for. Resist the temptation to fill the silences. People often need time to come up with just the right word.

- **Ask follow-up questions.** Your list of questions should serve as a road map that allows for detours. Often, people need to be prompted to fill in the gaps of their stories. Follow-up questions can be as easy as, then what happened? What else happened? How did that make you feel? What exactly do you mean when you say that? If your subject gives an incomplete answer to your question, try coming at the same question from a different angle.

- **Ask difficult questions.** People in mission work can encounter poignant or heart-wrenching situations that stir strong emotions, and this is an important part of their story. It's up to you to use compassion to draw out its telling. Remember that most people find it cathartic and healing to talk about upsetting experiences, and tears may be a natural part of the process.

- **Be attentive to accuracy.** Make sure you double-check titles, names, and dates, as well as the correct spelling of proper nouns. Always ask for a phone number or e-mail address in case you think of a question later that you forgot to ask.

- **Transcribe and edit your interviews.** Although this work can be time-consuming and tedious, written documents are easier to share and more convenient to use for future generations and historians.

1   Bette Buschow, interview by Nancy Kruh, January 23, 2012.
2   Dave Knapp, interview by Nancy Kruh, March 6, 2012.
3   Jenni Yeoh, interview by Nancy Kruh, March 7, 2012.
4   Robin Ball, interview by Nancy Kruh, March 1, 2012.
5   "The Summons," *The Faith We Sing* (Nashville, Abingdon Press, 2000), 2130.
6   Jeff Murrell, interview by Nancy Kruh, January 30, 2012.
7   Debbie Humphrey, interview by Nancy Kruh, January 20, 2012.
8   Debbie Humphrey, interview by Nancy Kruh, January 20, 2012.
9   Rosangela Soares de Oliveira, interview by Nancy Kruh, April 10, 2012.
10 Bethany Edwards-Goff, interview by Nancy Kruh, February 28, 2012.
11 Marcia Bent, interview by Nancy Kruh, January 25, 2012.
12 Cathy Mejia, interview by Nancy Kruh, February 28, 2012.
13 Cathy Mejia, interview by Nancy Kruh, February 28, 2012.
14 Brendan Kleiboer, interview by Nancy Kruh, March 8, 2012.
15 Debby Campbell, interview by Nancy Kruh, February 29, 2012.
16 Jessica Johnson, interview by Nancy Kruh, March 4, 2012.

CHAPTER 5

Living into the Kin-dom

By Nancy Kruh

As you read the preceding stories of these modern-day disciples, were you struck by how their words and actions seemed to resonate with the tenets of sacramental living? Being the one who gathered these accounts, I could say I planned it that way. But if I did, I wouldn't be doing justice to my own sense of discovery as I talked to these faithful Christians.

They hail from different generations, backgrounds, vocations, economic circumstances, and locales. Yet, as they each described their callings to me, I couldn't help but be awestruck by how they spoke such a similar language. Whether or not they knew scripture or the teachings of Wesley, I was moved, time and again, to hear in their voices the same echoes and refrains of Christ and of Methodism's founder.

How could this be? I think the answer is simple: to truly understand what it means to be a Christian—to embrace God's claim on our lives at a cellular level—we can't remain stationary. It is not enough to *be*. We must also *become*. And by its very nature, becoming requires transformative action.

As I conducted the interviews, I was struck as well by the interplay between these people's lives and the monumental ministries of our two spiritual role models. Just as the stories of these real-life people bring to light the teachings of Christ and Wesley, so do the teachings magnify the stories.

How, for example, can we not hear the vows of baptism resonate in these people's calls? Who among them isn't working to "serve as Christ's representatives in the world"? Whether it's Robin Ball directing Mission u (School of Christian Mission), Jeff Murrell spreading the gospel of environmental stewardship, Marcia Bent performing a Bible story, or Brendan Kleiboer studying to one day become a pediatrician, all of these people are striking out to be forces of good in the world. But the task of doing good also implies opposing forces are at play—a counterpoint made explicitly clear in the baptismal vows, as Chapter 1 has reminded us:

> Do you accept the freedom and power God gives you
> to resist evil, injustice, and oppression
> in whatever forms they present themselves?[1]

Bette Buschow's day-to-day work may be consumed with the particulars of the jail inmates her Dallas organization serves, but she never loses sight of the root causes that have created in the United States the largest incarceration rate in the world. Her compassion for the inmates is mingled with a "holy anger" directed at an unjust system that has failed these women at almost every turn: Many have attended substandard public schools that didn't teach basic skills, dooming them to a life of low-paying jobs and unemployment. Many have come from dysfunctional families of origin that were breeding grounds for physical and sexual abuse, as well as substance abuse. The cycle of abuse often has continued with toxic adult relationships and marriages. Crime becomes an all-too-common outgrowth of these circumstances. Once the women are back out on the streets, their plight only worsens. Jobs are even more scarce, alcohol and drugs can be a greater temptation to dull the pain, and their criminal records deny them access to any sort of government safety net—even food stamps.

"I simply didn't realize what we're doing with our zeal for incarceration," Buschow told me. "For some women, their only crime—so to speak—is that they're addicted and poor and abused. Look at whom Jesus interacted with and preached about. It's the poor, the ill, the ones who are in prison. That permeates all the way through the Gospels. These women are basically the same group of people who were around 2,000 years ago. We sure haven't made that much progress, have we?"[2]

GRASPING THE BIG PICTURE

In her community organizing work in Phoenix, Jessica Johnson can easily connect the dots between the personal and the political. When she knocks on doors, looking for candidates for job training programs, she comes face-to-face with the human stories behind sterile news reports about unemployment and economic disparity. Often she meets people who don't get enough to eat, struggle to pay their utility bills, and don't have access to anything but emergency room medical care. Though Johnson has learned from experience that churches and other nonprofit entities can make a big difference, she also realizes "there are limits to what charity can do. There are so many complex barriers to success, to stability, to health, and to having enough to eat. If we don't work on systemic problems, we're not getting anywhere. You can't ensure that all are fed and all are a part of the community without speaking to the powers that prevent that from happening."[3]

Johnson and Buschow impressed me with their ability to see the bigger picture, but they impressed me even more with their refusal to yield to discouragement. After all, the bigger picture is as overwhelming as it is awesome.

The two women also moved me for their refusal to bow to complacency. At some point in their lives, they accepted the metaphorical challenge that was raised in Chapter 2: Which Holy Week procession into Jerusalem will you join, Caesar's or Jesus'? How much easier it is to simply accept the status quo, perhaps even cheer it on because, "that's the way it's always been." But Christ beckons us to model the boldness he displayed when he implicated a corrupt empire for its role in human suffering.

Here we are, more than two millennia later, and we're still enduring the predictable consequences of global greed, oppression, and indifference. Then as now, the human race resides amid a massive web of power structures and institutions that hold terrible sway in the world. But as small as we may feel, each of us still occupies a strand in that web, and our actions have the capacity to reverberate. We increase that capacity by joining forces with others in the magnificent array of groups and organizations dedicated to righting the world's wrongs. Chapter 3 offered us a thoughtful list of avenues for engagement at every level of society, and it's worth noting that all the people profiled in Chapter 4 are living out their calling through some sort of church group or agency. "Never believe that a few caring people can't change the world," cultural anthropologist Margaret Mead famously said, "for, indeed, that's all who ever have."[4]

Our baptism is intended to empower us. With the force field of God's "amazing grace," we can fearlessly commit ourselves to joining in God's mission. We are called to be optimists: our faith allows us to believe that we can make an impact.

"What you can't do as one person, even a small group can make larger steps toward change," Johnson said. "Playing your little role in that bigger project can be amazing."

GOD'S DESTINY FOR US

If baptism gives us our "marching orders" that send us out into the world, then Holy Communion reveals the destiny that God intends for us. Living sacramentally and walking justly isn't just about "doing good." Nor is it only about fighting evil. Above all, it is a transformative act that moves us in the direction of God's promised kin-dom.

Throughout scripture, we are given tantalizing—and often mysterious—clues to what this kin-dom is. Isaiah tells us how "**The wolf shall live with the lamb, the leopard shall lie down with the kid, the calf and the lion and the fatling together, and a little child shall lead them**" (Isaiah 11:6). Amos foresees "when the one who plows shall overtake the one who reaps, and the treader of grapes the one who sows the seed" (Amos 9:13).

Though Old Testament prophecy seems to predict a universally acknowledged Messiah would someday appear to begin God's holy reign, Christ left his followers with too much evidence to believe the Son of God could somehow magically deliver that day in their time. Just listening to Jesus' descriptions of the kin-dom, who could believe the world was already measuring up?

"Blessed are the meek, for they will inherit the earth" (Matthew 5:5).

"The last will be first, and the first will be last" (Matthew 20:16).

"And all who exalt themselves will be humbled, and those who humble themselves will be exalted" (Matthew 23:12).

Jesus was the great practitioner of paradox, and he delivered among his most intriguing after the Pharisees asked him when God's promised reign would begin. It "is not something that can be observed," he said, "nor will people say, 'here it is,' or 'there it is' " (Luke 17:20–21). But then he added, it already "is in your midst."

In the light of this pronouncement, Holy Communion takes on profound significance. Consider how the "real world" is turned upside down by the Eucharist: All are invited, and all are nourished. Division is erased. Dissension ceases. As we humble ourselves at the altar to share equally in Christ's sacrifice, love and justice prevail.

In those few precious moments, as Johnson described it to me, we witness "a model for the way the world ought to be: that everyone is fed and no one is turned away." She is grateful that she attends a church that serves Communion each Sunday, so that weekly she can experience a taste of "salvation, an equal world where we're all welcome."[5]

Yes, it is symbolic of what can be—and yet it is also immediate. Simultaneously, this is the *already here* and the *not yet*. Christ's paradox is made real at the table.

Considering the world's problems, it's almost too much to grasp that God's kin-dom could be within our reach. After all, what would our everyday lives look like in a world of Holy Communion where love and justice prevail? The Shangri-Las and utopias of literature conjure up a scene of constant smiles and endless harmony, where the masses wander about, mindlessly exchanging the passing of the peace. Our own imaginations may have difficulty going beyond this lollipop-and-sunshine view.

But theologian Paul Tillich rejects this superficial understanding. Upending exploitation and economic injustice doesn't mean that productivity and creativity would cease. Rooting out the greed and selfishness in our leadership wouldn't be an end to governing systems. Putting a stop to armed conflict doesn't keep revolutionary change from occurring. Taking to heart all the lessons that God teaches us doesn't mean that there's no longer room for spiritual growth. Otherwise, Tillich posits, life would turn into insufferable monotony. He imagines this world as a place where "the dynamics of life and, with it, life itself would have come to an end. . . . Nothing is risked, everything is decided. Life has ceased to transcend itself."[6]

God's kin-dom is not a stagnant place. It still bustles with transformation—the sort that can be found wherever God's call is answered in this troubled world today. Indeed, what would the world look like if it were blanketed by a global movement of sacramental living? Let's revisit some of our modern-day disciples as they live out their call, and see if we can catch a clearer glimpse of the coming kin-dom.

OUT OF GRATITUDE, NOT OBLIGATION

What does the Lord require of us? (Micah 6:8a).

It is among the most crucial questions posed in scripture, and it is laden with a sense of obligation. But obligation need not be laden with joylessness. People who embrace God's claim on their lives overflow with gratitude. "Should do" is transformed into "want to do."

Reflecting on his acts of discipleship, Dave Knapp abhors the idea of "obligation."

"I feel it's why God put us on this earth," the disaster-relief team leader told me. "I have to make a decision that glorifies God in every way. I have no choice. I'm convicted in my spirit. Doing God's will every day, the chaos is gone, and joy takes its place."[7]

Q1   Do I Identify with Jonah?
        In what way?

Q2   What are the reasons we don't want
to do what God is asking for?

Q3   Have you ever turned the other way?
Or been silent and not responded to
something God was calling you to do?

Knapp's gladness resounded again and again in the words of the others I talked with. It was put there not only by their faith that they are following God's will, but also by their total immersion into community—the "kin" in kin-dom. Living sacramentally means spurning the patriarchal paradigm of the helper and the helpless, and instead putting ourselves on equal footing with the people we are in service with. It means shunning the "us versus them" mentality and recognizing humanity's architecture of interdependence. It means offering, not a handout, but our very selves.

To me, no one exemplifies these values more than Buschow, who built the foundation of her ministry on her realization that she wasn't all that different from the women she met in prison. "The threads of commonality between us have always been at the forefront for me," she said. "We are much more alike than different."[8]

Buschow harbors "a very strong resistance" to calling the women "broken people," and instead thinks of them as "representatives of what's broken in our world. They're people who simply haven't recognized God in themselves and the potential that they have."[9]

Debbie Humphrey can also see herself in the Native American youth who come to the Oklahoma community center where she works. Like many of them, she grew up poor and hungry for love and guidance in a home that offered mostly abuse and neglect. But Humphrey also sees God in the faces of these young people. "I stand on Matthew 25:40 that when you do to others, you do to me," she said. "Hopefully and prayerfully, they see God in me. I start out my prayers, 'God help me to see you and help them to see you through me.'"[10]

GIVING AND RECEIVING

While living sacramentally can be demanding, it doesn't require putting on sackcloth and ashes—a hard lesson even for those committed to responding to God's call. Among those I talked to, some seemed to still have "old tapes" playing from a strict upbringing that taught them mission work is a grim act missionary. "I couldn't hold back my tears," she said. "That is where it started, how I became a Christian. What a privilege to put my hands on her shoulder and send her out to do what someone like her did for me."[19]

"KEEP YOUR EYES ON THE PRIZE"

As this study comes to a close, the time has come to envision the future God has in store and to imagine ourselves as an active part of it.

It's a task that reminds me of one of the great anthems of the Civil Rights Movement, a song called "Keep Your Eyes on the Prize." Civil rights workers endured tremendous trials: arrests, beatings, harassment, death threats, assassinations. There must have been many, many days when they wondered if one more sit-in, march, or voter registration drive would make a difference. But through it all, the anthem's refrain urged, "Keep your eyes on the prize, hold on." Martin Luther King Jr.'s "I Have a Dream" speech was a compelling description of that "prize" of freedom, justice, and equality. It's no coincidence that much of the basis for his dream came from the book that first offered the hope of a promised land.

Having a vision, a precious dream, is essential to doing God's work. It keeps us focused, optimistic, and mindful that we are part of something greater than ourselves. What does your vision look like, and what will be your role in it? How will you be called to act on God's promise of love, justice, and peace? Who and what do you want to *become*?

The intent of the preceding chapters has been to offer both theological underpinning and concrete guidance to help you respond to these questions and set you on the path of faith.

Chapter 1 has shown how baptism and Holy Communion reinforce God's claim on us, reminding us of God's capacity to love, to heal, and to transform. With gratitude, we can welcome the knowledge that we aren't merely bystanders in this world. We are invited to join in God's ongoing creation, and we have exquisite directions on how to do so from the life and teachings of Christ.

Chapter 2 has told how all encompassing our task is. Living sacramentally is both a personal and a public commitment to transformation. We cannot do it alone—but Wesley teaches us that we don't have to. We are the recipients of the unearned and undeserved gift of God's amazing grace, which empowers us with God's gifts and equips us as disciples. Wesley shows us how to access the full potential of this "grace sufficient" through "works of piety": studying scripture, prayer, fasting, Christian conferencing and conversation, Holy Communion and worship.

Chapter 3 has detailed the many ways we can undertake what Wesley considered "works of mercy." God is calling us to be the hands and feet of Christ, to be sent out into the world in mission and ministry. How can we become part of God's kin-dom movement? How can we help bring wholeness to this broken world? It is our charge to listen for God's call, to discern it, and to respond.

The individual accounts featured in Chapter 4 have shown us what it means to act on our faith, and they have revealed the joy of transformation that can come from following God's call. When we reach outside ourselves, when we shed our self-interests for God's priorities, we receive the opportunity to become change agents—and to be changed ourselves.

HARDWIRED TO RESPOND

Perhaps no greater models for responding to God's call are brothers Simon and Andrew, who dropped their fishing nets—and everything else in their lives—and came simply because Jesus beckoned (Mark 1:14–20). Can it ever be that easy?

Author and preacher Barbara Brown Taylor asks the same question, suggesting most people who hear this Gospel story "start worrying about whether they have what it takes to be a disciple."[20] But Taylor doesn't credit the actions of these fledgling followers on any burst of courage.

"If you ask me, this is not a hero story but a miracle story . . ." she says. "This is a story about God, and about God's ability not only to call us but also to create us as people who are able to follow."

God's ability to create us as people who are able to follow. Intriguingly, Taylor's description is reflected in a relatively new scientific inquiry that is trying to find a genetic basis for selfless behavior. Even as evolutionist Charles Darwin was formulating his theories about natural selection, he was well aware that the powerful forces of self-preservation flew in the face of the undeniable existence of altruism—not just in humans, but in animals and insects as well.

"If Nature was bloody in tooth and claw. . . how could a behavior that *lowered* fitness be selected?" science historian Oren Harman writes. "Survival of the fittest or survival of the nicest: It was a conundrum the Darwinians would need to solve."[21]

A lively scientific debate continues today over the "origin of kindness." But while scientists try to unravel the particulars of the matter, I dare say that we as Christians can grasp the mystery. Doubtless, part of our makeup is the tug we feel toward our own needs, but we know there is also something in our very nature that is hardwired to respond to the world's needs. *This is who we are: God has created us as people who are able to follow.*

Taylor goes on to point out that in "that God-drenched moment" when Peter and Andrew dropped everything, "the miracle occurred: their lives flowed in the same direction of God's life. . . . Time was fulfilled. The [kin-dom] came—and comes—every time our own lives are brought into the same flow, so that we, too, allow ourselves to fall in love and follow God, and can do no other."[22]

This is what Taylor calls the "miracle of discipleship," and it is unfurled in "a different story for every one of us in our own particular lives."[23]

This is who you are: God has created you as a person who is able to follow. Isn't that really all you need to know to go?

1   "The Baptismal Covenant IV," *The United Methodist Hymnal* (Nashville, The United Methodist Publishing House, 1993), 50.

2   Bette Buschow, interview by Nancy Kruh, January 23, 2012.

3   Jessica Johnson, interview by Nancy Kruh, March 4, 2012.

4   Elayne Clift, *Women, Philanthropy, and Social Change: Visions for a Just Society* (University Press of New England, Lebanon, New Hampshire), 212

5   Jessica Johnson, interview by Nancy Kruh, March 4, 2012.

6   Paul Tillich, "The Unity of Love, Power, and Justice," *The Essential Tillich: An Anthology of the Writings of Paul Tillich* (The University of Chicago Press, Chicago, 1987), 156.

7   Dave Knapp, interview by Nancy Kruh, March 6, 2012.

8   Bette Buschow, interview by Nancy Kruh, March 4, 2012.

9   Ibid.

10 Debbie Humphrey, interview by Nancy Kruh, January 20, 2012.

11 Bette Buschow, interview.

12 Jenni Yeoh, interview by Nancy Kruh, March 7, 2012.

13 Rosangela Oliveira, interview by Nancy Kruh, April 10, 2012.

14 Brendan Kleiboer, interview by Nancy Kruh, March 8, 2012.

15 Debbie Humphrey, interview.

16 Jessica Johnson, interview.

17 Rosangela Oliveira, interview.

18 Jenni Yeoh, interview.

19 Ibid.

20 Barbara Brown Taylor, "Miracle on the Beach," *Home By Another Way* (Cowley Publications, Boston, 1999), 37–41.

21 Oren Harman, *The Price of Altruism: George Price and the Search for the Origins of Kindness,* (W.W. Norton & Company, New York, 2010), 3.

22 Barbara Brown Taylor, "Miracle on the Beach," 37–41.

23 Ibid.

Bibliography

"Articles of Religion of the Methodist Church." *The Book of Discipline of the United Methodist Church, 2008.* Nashville: Abingdon Press, 2008, ¶103. Section 3.

Bolton, Nick. "Resolving to Practice Some iPhone Abstinence." *The New York Times.* January 2, 2012, sec. B.

Borg, Marcus J. *Putting Away Childish Things: A Tale of Modern Faith.* New York: HarperOne, 2010.

Borg, Marcus J. and John Dominic Crossan. *The Last Week: What the Gospels Really Teach About Jesus's Final Days in Jerusalem.* New York: HarperCollins, 2006.

Bredthauer, Donald. "Community Organizing for a Just Response to Violence." Quoted in William K. McElvaney, *Becoming a Justice Seeking Congregation: Responding to God's Justice Initiative.* New York, Bloomington: iUniverse, Inc., 2009.

Buechner, Frederick. *Wishful Thinking: A Seeker's ABC.* San Francisco: Harper San Francisco, 1993.

"By Water and the Spirit," Resolution 8013. *The Book of Resolutions of the United Methodist Church, 2008.* Nashville: Abingdon Press, 2008.

Caldwell, Neill and Linda Rhodes. "Black and Red All Over: Virginia United Methodist Day at the General Assembly." *Faith in Action,* February 13, 2012. http://www.umc-gbcs.org/site/apps/nlnet/content.as px?c=frLJK2PKLqF&b=7981347&ct=11627327.

Clift, Elayne. *Women, Philanthropy, and Social Change: Visions for a Just Society.* Lebanon, New Hampshire: University Press of New England, 2007.

Connor, Jessica. "Wrapped in Prayer: Quilts Comfort Those in Need." *United Methodist Reporter.* January 5, 2010, 4B.

Day, Katie. *Difficult Conversations: Taking Risks, Acting with Integrity.* Alban Publishing, 2001.

Driver, Tom F. *The Magic of Ritual: Our Need for Liberating Rites that Transform Our Lives and Our Communities.* New York: Harper Collins Publishers, 1991.

Edwards, Tilden. *Spiritual Friend: Reclaiming the Gift of Spiritual Direction.* Mahwah, NJ: Paulist Press, 1980.

Ehrman, Bart D. *The New Testament: A Historical Introduction to the Early Christian Writings.* New York, Oxford: Oxford University Press, 2008.

Felton, Gayle Carlton. *By Water and the Spirit.* Nashville: Discipleship Resources, 1996.

———. *This Holy Mystery: A United Methodist Understanding of Holy Communion.* Nashville: Discipleship Resources, 2005.

Finger, Reta Halteman. *Roman House Churches for Today: A Practical Guide for Small Groups.* Grand Rapids: William B. Eerdmann's Publishing, 2007.

Floyd, Charlene. *Christian Voices: Journeys Through Faith and Politics in Contemporary American Protestantism.* Westport, CT: Praeger Publishers, 2007.

Gilbert, Kathy. "From Poverty to Family: Program Makes Room at Table for the Poor." *United Methodist Reporter.* January 13, 2012, 1Aff.

Gonzalez, Catherine Gunsalus and Justo L. Gonzalez. *For the Love of God: The Epistles of John.* New York: United Methodist Women, 2010.

"Guidelines for Holy Conferencing – What God Expects of Us." The People of the United Methodist Church. The United Methodist Church. Accessed May 25, 2012. www.umc.org/atf/cf/%7Bdb6a45e4-c446-4248-82c8-e131b6424741%7D/GUIDELINESFORCHRISTIAN-CONFERENCING5.PDF.

Hawking, C.J. "A People's Cathedral in Wisconsin." **response**. April 2011.

Horsley, Richard A. *The Liberation of Christmas: The Infancy Narratives in Social Context.* New York: Crossroads Publishing, 1989.

"I Was There to Hear Your Borning Cry." *The Faith We Sing.* Nashville: Abingdon Press, 2000.

Knotts, Alice G. "Thelma Stevens, Crusader for Racial Justice." Quoted in Rosemary Skinner Keller, *Spirituality and Social Ministry: Vocational Vision of Women in the United Methodist Tradition.* Nashville: Abingdon Press, 1993.

Kruh, Nancy. *The Disciple Story: The Transforming Power of Scripture.* Nashville: Abingdon Press, 2003.

Lehrer, Jonah. "Kin and Kind." *The New Yorker.* March 5, 2012.

Martin, Dale B. *The Corinthian Body*. New Haven and London: Yale University Press, 1995.

Martin, James. *Between Heaven and Mirth: Why Joy, Humor and Laughter Are at the Heart of the Spiritual Life*. New York: HarperOne, 2011.

McClain, George D. *Claiming All Things for God: Prayer, Discernment and Ritual for Social Change*. Nashville, Abingdon Press, 1998.

Moreton, Alan. "Church's Small Group Dedicated to Study of Science and Theology." *United Methodist Reporter*. January 6, 2012, 2B.

Norberg, Tilda. *Consenting to Grace: An Introduction to Gestalt Pastoral Care*. Staten Island, NY: Penn House Press, 2006.

———. *Gathered Together: Creating Personal Liturgies for Healing and Transformation*. Nashville: Upper Room Books, 2007.

Oates, Stephen B. *Let the Trumpet Sound: The Life of Martin Luther King, Jr.* New York: Harper and Row Publishers, 1982.

Olsen, Charles M. *Transforming Church Boards into Communities of Spiritual Leaders*. Alban Publishing, 1995.

Olson, Lynne. *Freedom's Daughters: The Unsung Heroines of the Civil Rights Movement from 1830–1970*. New York: Scribner, 2001.

Taylor, Barbara Brown. "Miracle on the Beach." *Home By Another Way*. Boston: Cowley Publications, 1999.

"This Holy Mystery: A United Methodist Understanding of Holy Communion," Resolution 8014. *The Book of Resolutions of the United Methodist Church, 2008*. Nashville: Abingdon Press, 2008.

Tillich, Paul. "The Unity of Love, Power, and Justice." *The Essential Tillich: An Anthology of the Writings of Paul Tillich*. Chicago: The University of Chicago Press, 1987.

The United Methodist Book of Discipline 2008. Nashville: Abingdon Press, 2008.

The United Methodist Hymnal. Nashville: The United Methodist Publishing House, 1989.

West Side Campaign Against Hunger. *2011 Annual Report*. www.wscah. org.

Wink, Walter. *Engaging the Powers: Discernment and Resistance in a World of Domination*. Minneapolis: Fortress Press, 1992.

———. *The Powers That Be: Theology for a New Millennium*. New York: Doubleday, 1998.

Young, Carlton. *Companion to the United Methodist Hymnal*. Nashville: Abingdon Press, 1993.

Yrigoyen, Jr., Charles. *John Wesley: Holiness of Heart and Life*. Nashville: Abingdon Press, 1996.

The Call: Living Sacramentally, Walking Justly

Participant's Guide
by Becky Dodson Louter and Pat Hoerth

Introduction

The intent for this guide is to provide individuals and groups spiritual tools to experience *The Call: Living Sacramentally, Walking Justly* more deeply. The exercises and tools presented here are to aid us on the journey. While we all want to start out running, it is helpful to remember the image of a child, who advances from rolling over as an infant, to crawling, to those first wobbly toddler steps, and then to running on legs that have been made strong and sturdy through the journey. In spiritual growth, we "strengthen our legs" by going back to the foundations of scripture and tradition, taking time to be alone with God to reflect and listen, so that we can go forth again. We need spiritual tools to help us ground ourselves in God and to discern where God is calling us at this point in our lives. This daily discipline will help us to engage justly in God's kin-dom—the term this text uses for God's egalitarian realm.

Our authors present great examples and tools to deepen our spirituality in the text. We hope the exercises and discussions presented in this guide's four sessions, as well as the expanded online version (www.unitedmethodistwomen.org), will augment your experience with the study. Deepening our understanding of the sacraments of baptism and Holy Communion will help us to walk justly, engaging in transformative action as individuals and communities.

Before you begin, you may want to choose a journal to use during this study as you further explore the text and experiences in this guide.

Session 1

God's Gift: Named and Claimed in Baptism

INTRODUCTION TO SESSION 1

The first two sessions of the Participant's Guide are companions to Chapter 1 in the study. The first session, about baptism, connects with pages 10–18. The second session, on Holy Communion, connects with pages 18–27.

> At its heart, baptism is a bold act. We are marked with God's stamp that echoes the very story of creation: "God saw everything that he had made, and indeed, it was very good" (Genesis 1:31). God says a resounding yes to us in our baptism. Yes, I claim you as my own. Whatever happens to you, I will be there with you, seeking to redeem you, bringing you to your right mind, holding you in my arms, rejoicing in your beauty and uniqueness (p. 12)

McClain and Norberg write that the "covenant of baptism is a crucial channel of what we call the grace of God." The United Methodist Service for the Baptismal Covenant, presented in detail in Chapter 1, provides great clarity for the significance and connection that we are all called to represent Christ in walking justly. The goal of Session 1 is to engage in spiritual practices that invite us to bring the experience of our baptism to heart so that we will deeply know our belovedness and can commit, or recommit, to the baptismal covenant we make in community with God and God's kin-dom.

GATHERING

One Voice: We are a people of the water!

Many Voices: We worship God, whose love spilled forth and created this beautiful blue marble and water-rich planet that is our home.

One Voice: We are a people of the water!

Many Voices: We worship God, whose uncontainable love falls like rain, flows like a river, and fills the oceans.

One Voice: We are a people of the water!

Many Voices: We worship God, who through the water of our baptism showed us that we are loved.

One Voice: We are a people of the water!

Many Voices: We worship God, whose love bubbles up in our hearts and overflows into the hearts of others.

One Voice: We are a people of the water!

Many Voices: We worship God, whose love courses through our lives like the water that sustains all life, so that we may be life giving.

All Voices: The love of God is like water. The justice of God rolls down like waters. We are a people of the water!

SONG

Choose a song or hymn to be sung here.

OPENING PRAYER (IN UNISON)

Most amazing God, in these days together, may I more deeply understand my baptism and Holy Communion. May my life flow from them as a sacrament in which you are always present. Through your naming me in baptism and nourishing me in Communion, may I come to understand my common call to be love and justice in the world. Help me to understand the unique way I am to live that call.

Through this study, open me to a deeper understanding of the freedom and joy of life in you, O God, Creator, Sustainer, Life-Giver, Source of Justice. May I live sacramentally and walk justly. In Jesus' name I pray, Amen.

LECTIO DIVINA

Lectio divina literally means "divine reading" of a passage—from scripture or another writing. Follow these steps to read the above passage using *lectio divina*:

1. Slowly read the passage aloud simply to hear it.

2. Slowly read the passage aloud again and listen for a word or phrase that strikes you. Notice the word or phrase that gets your attention.

3. Slowly read the passage aloud a third time and then ask God to show you its meaning for you at this time. Be silent with an attitude of listening. Write in a journal the word or phrase and its meaning for you today.

SCRIPTURE: THE BAPTISM OF JESUS, MARK 1:9—11

Read the passage using *lectio divina* to hear what God is saying to you today.

> In those days Jesus came from Nazareth of Galilee and was baptized
> by John in the Jordan. And just as he was coming up out of the water,
> he saw the heavens torn apart and the Spirit descending like a dove on
> him. And a voice came from heaven, "You are my Son, the Beloved;
> with you I am well pleased."

EXPLORING SCRIPTURE THROUGH OUR IMAGINATION

One of the prayer methods the text authors list in their sidebar "How to
Enrich Your Prayer Life" is imaginative prayer (p. 54). Using our God-
given imaginations, we can be with Jesus as John baptizes him in the
Jordan River. Slowly and prayerfully follow the script, or if you are in a
group, listen as the facilitator reads it to you.

Imagine yourself, at the River Jordan. Burdened by life's challenges,
you have come away from the city and traveled out into the wilderness
with others. You've heard that there is a man who is dipping people in
the river and helping them reclaim their closeness with God. That sounds
hopeful to you, so you have come to the river. Smell the clean desert air.
Does it smell dry? Dusty? Spicy? Sweet?

(Pause)

See the water. Notice its color. Is it blue and clear? Is it muddy?
(Pause)

Hear the breeze as it blows through the scrubby trees alongside the river.
Can you hear the water moving in the river? Listen for the hushed voices
around the river and see John, in the water, holding people and dunking
them in the river water.

(Pause)

Hear the splash of water as another person rises out of the river, wipes her face, and slogs in her heavy clothing back to the shore.

(Pause)

You watch and consider if you are willing to walk into the water yourself. Notice how you are feeling. Do you want to go into the river, too? Are you resistant? Are you apprehensive but feeling drawn to the water anyway? Are you eager?

(Pause)

Then one man goes into the river and walks toward John. Your attention is drawn to him. Maybe it's the way he approaches John or the expression on his face. Maybe it's the expression on John's face as he sees this man.

(Pause)

The man and John seem to have an exchange, and then John lowers him into the water. John raises him out of the water and you notice something different about the man. A certain feeling comes over you. What are you feeling?

(Pause)
You watch as the man comes ashore and walks along the riverbank until you can see him no more.

(Pause)

For some reason, you don't hesitate now, but walk into the water and approach John. John places his hands on your back and your head and lowers you into the water. Suddenly, you are springing up out of the water and are overcome with a sensation that you've never felt before. You hear a tender voice saying to you: "You are my child, my Beloved." You hear your name spoken: "_____, with you I am well pleased."

(Long Pause)

You somehow find that you have made it back to shore and you sit there on the bank, letting the sun and warm air dry you. You allow this experience to soak deeply into your being. You keep hearing the words, "You are my child, my Beloved." You hear your name: "_____, with you I am well pleased."

(Long Pause)

REFLECT
Write about your experience with this imaginative prayer:

- What did you experience?
- What impact did this prayer have on you?
- How did this imaginative prayer inform your understanding of baptism?

In the Methodist tradition, sprinkling, pouring, or immersion have been allowed as modes of baptism. We believe that baptism is by water and the Holy Spirit. The congregation affirms it as full participants, not as onlookers, when a person is baptized.

CONNECTING THE SCRIPTURE TO OUR STORIES

In the text, our authors write:

> At its heart, baptism is a bold act. We are marked with God's stamp that echoes the very story of creation: "God saw everything that he had made, and indeed, it was very good" (Genesis 1:31). God says a resounding yes to us in our baptism. Yes, I claim you as my own. (p. 12)

Your birth story, your naming story, your baptism story, if you have one, are part of your story with God. Reflecting on them helps enlarge and enliven your experience of hearing God say to you: "_____ you are my Beloved."

"We are the beloved. We are intimately loved long before our parents, teachers, spouses, children, and friends loved or wounded us. That's the truth of our lives. That's the truth spoken by the voice that says, 'You are my Beloved.'"[1]

Consider the circumstance of your birth: time, place, season, your parents and grandparents, and any siblings. Think about the name you were given at your baptism: first, middle, last, and any nicknames. Think about the circumstances surrounding your name; its origin in your family or culture, and what your name means. Reflect on how you feel about your name and that this is what you have been called all your life.

CONNECTING OUR STORY WITH GOD TO THE CHURCH COMMUNITY: THE COVENANT

Now that we have remembered our belovedness and God's grace in claiming and naming us, what is our response? At the time of our baptism, our church family and loved ones brought us into covenant with God and one another, just as our biblical ancestors did. God initiated the covenant and gave us the grace to accept the promise of being faithful to God and one another. (See the discussion of our baptismal covenant in the text, pages 10–18.)

Read Larry's baptismal story that begins on page 10. Your story is undoubtedly different. Take a moment to journal about your baptism experience. As you write, remember that there are no "right" answers, only the answer that reflects what you truly believe. Think about the qualifiers you use in your answers. Reflect and write about your feelings and thoughts that best express your present state.

REFLECT

If you have been baptized, consider the following questions:

- What was your baptism like?
- Have you taken part in any service of reaffirmation of faith where you were asked to "Remember your baptism and be thankful"?
- What does the covenant mean to you now?
- What would your life look like if every day you were aware of living as God's beloved one?
- How does your life look if you are aware that God has named you, claimed you, and asked you to be love in the world?

If you have not been baptized, consider the following questions:

- What is your story as to why you were not baptized?
- How do you want to respond to being God's beloved?
- What would it mean to you to be baptized today?

RECOGNIZING THE CALL IN OUR BAPTISMAL COVENANT

In our text, we read:

> We are graced by God with the gift of making decisions. We are called to join in God's mission to resist what is not of God. How often we resign ourselves to injustice, thinking we are powerless! Our baptismal vows do not allow us to wallow in self-pity or our own perceived weakness, to give up in the face of what harms human life. Nor can we just give in to our own destructive patterns and compulsions. We don't stop seeking God's healing. We are never to reject the "freedom and power God gives you." Wesley called this the imperative of "holy living." In other words, we are called to walk justly! And in doing so, we place ourselves in the force field of God's "amazing grace." (p. 17)

Realize the power of your baptism more deeply as you consider the following questions:

- Do you hear in our baptismal covenant the responsibility to pay attention to injustice that results from "the evil powers of this world"?

- Can you recognize God's call to face the forms of systemic injustice that we are part of?

- Can you accept baptism as a source of power to "resist evil and injustice?"

LECTIO DIVINA WITH THE BAPTISMAL COVENANT

> *Do you renounce the spiritual forces of wickedness,*
> *reject the evil powers of this world,*
> *and repent of your sin?*[2]

Use the *lectio divina* three-step process to pray with this part of our baptismal covenant: listen to the words, let a word or phrase strike you, and ask God to reveal its meaning for you today. Record your experience with this prayer in your journal.

In the light of this passage, are there other promises you want to make with God and the church to be God's love and justice in the world? Write a letter to the Creator, Jesus, and/or the Holy Spirit expressing your heart-felt covenant—your promises—to live out your God-given belovedness on earth at this time in your life.

CLOSING

Dip your fingers into a bowl of water, touch your heart and pray your gratitude: "Thank you, most gracious God for reminding me that I am your beloved, _____(name)."

Offer your letter of covenant to God. "I covenant with you, O most gracious God, and with the church to _____ _____."

CLOSING HYMN

I Was There to Hear Your Borning Cry (*The Faith We Sing*, no. 2051)

HOMEWORK

Read Chapter 1 of the text.

---

1   Henri Nouwen, *Life of the Beloved: Spiritual Living in a Secular World* (New York: Crossroad, 1992), 36.
2   "Congregational Reaffirmation of the Baptismal Covenant," *The United Methodist Hymnal,* (Nashville, Abingdon Press, 1993), 50.

Session 2

God's Gift: Nourished and Sustained in Holy Communion

Sometimes celebrated in secrecy amid political oppression, cruelty and injustice, Holy Communion shines with a radical message of justice and dignity for all people. All are welcome here; all are fed. Around this table, the kin-dom is already come and God's will is being done on earth as it is in heaven. (p. 23)

INTRODUCTION

Session 2 is based on pages 18–28 in the text. Participants are invited to renew and deepen their experience of Holy Communion with Christ, for it is that sustenance that enables the body of Christ to continue its call to live the covenant of walking justly every day of their lives.

GATHERING

ONE VOICE: God is with us in the vastness of the night sky, the translucent beauty of a lacewing butterfly, the elegance of a leaping gazelle, the magnificence of the Sierra Nevada Mountains.

MANY VOICES: God is really with us.

ONE VOICE: God is with us in the hospital room, the jail cell, the violent home, at the deathbed, and in the throes of divorce.

MANY VOICES: God is really with us.

ONE VOICE: God is with us at the table—in the church sanctuary, in our homes, at the soup kitchen, and in the school cafeteria.

MANY VOICES: God is really with us.

ONE VOICE: God is with us in the struggle for justice, in the seeking of reconciliation. God is with us as we sit with those who have disappointed or betrayed us, and as we stand with those who have no voice in our society.

MANY VOICES: God is really with us.

ONE VOICE: In the bread, in the wine, in the body of Christ, in the beloved community,

MANY VOICES: We remember: God is really with us.

SONG

One Bread One Body (*The United Methodist Hymnal*, no. 620)

OPENING PRAYER (IN UNISON)

Most gracious God, your love for us is astounding. We see it all around us in your creation. We feel your loving Spirit in our hearts, and we know your call to us through the life and teachings of Jesus of Nazareth. We are freshly aware of your grace given in baptism. We are freshly recommitted to live as a covenantal people. We come now to study what it means to be at the table with you. Through this study, deepen our understanding, so that we may be in loving communion with you, one another, and with all of your creation. In Jesus' name we pray, Amen.

SCRIPTURE STUDY: THE LAST SUPPER, LUKE 22:7—20

Use *lectio divina* to read this passage and write in a journal the word or phrase that stands out to you and its meaning for you today.

> Then came the day of Unleavened Bread, on which the Passover lamb had to be sacrificed. So Jesus sent Peter and John, saying, "Go and prepare the Passover meal for us that we may eat it." They asked him, "Where do you want us to make preparations for it?" "Listen," he said to them, "when you have entered the city, a man carrying a jar of water will meet you; follow him into the house he enters and say to the owner of the house, 'The teacher asks you, "Where is the guest room, where I may eat the Passover with my disciples?"' He will show you a large room upstairs, already furnished. Make preparations for us there." So they went and found everything as he had told them; and they prepared the Passover meal. When the hour came, he took his place at the table, and the apostles with him. He said to them, "I have eagerly desired to eat this Passover with you before I suffer; for I tell you, I will not eat it until it is fulfilled in the kingdom of God." Then he took a cup, and after giving thanks he said, "Take this and divide it among yourselves; for I tell you that from now on I will not drink of the fruit of the vine until the kingdom of God comes." Then he took a loaf of bread, and when he had given thanks, he broke it and gave it to them, saying, "This is my body, which is given for you.

Do this in remembrance of me." And he did the same with the cup after supper, saying, "This cup that is poured out for you is the new covenant in my blood."

EXPLORING SCRIPTURE THROUGH OUR IMAGINATION

Slowly and prayerfully follow the script presented here, or, if you are in a group, relax and listen as the facilitator reads it to you, entering into the story with your imagination.

Jerusalem is busy. It's Passover, the time when pilgrims come to the city to remember that God led Moses to bring the Hebrew people out of captivity in Egypt. Jesus of Nazareth has made arrangements for this Passover meal. The room is furnished with cushions and carpets and a low, U-shaped table at which the disciples will recline for the meal. The wine, unleavened bread, and bitter herbs are already provided. Peter and John sacrificed the lamb at the temple, slitting the lamb's throat at the appropriate time during the liturgy. It has been roasted on a pomegranate wood spit. The lamps have been filled.

When all is prepared and the lamps in the dark room are lit, Jesus joins the disciples. Imagine the private gathering in this dark but warmly lit room.

(Pause)

Notice the colors of the cushions and carpets.

(Pause)

See the faces of the disciples. Notice their robes, their sandals left at the door, the wine, and plates of food.

(Pause)

Imagine how they greet one another as they enter.

(Pause)

Smell the combination of scents: lamp oil, roasted lamb, and bitter herbs.

(Pause)

See Jesus there with them. How does he look? What is his demeanor? How does he interact with his friends?

(Pause)

Observe them as they recline around the low table. What is the mood in the room? Are they laughing and talking? Are they subdued?

(Pause)

Imagine the tension in the room as Jesus says: "I have eagerly desired to eat this Passover with you before I suffer, for I tell you, I will not eat it again until it is fulfilled in the kingdom of God."

(Pause)

Watch as Jesus takes a cup, gives thanks for it, and tells those at the table to divide it among themselves. Watch as each of the disciples drinks from the cup.

(Pause)

Then see him take the loaf of unleavened bread—the symbol of the old covenant between God and the Hebrew people—and give thanks for it. Watch as he breaks the bread, as is the custom during the Passover meal, and then say this surprising thing: "This is *my body* which is given for you. Do this in remembrance of me."

(Pause)

Watch the faces of the disciples as they pass the flat bread and eat it, having heard Jesus' words. What is the mood in the room now? What do the faces of the disciples show you?

Pause)

After supper, see Jesus take the cup and say: "This cup that is poured out for you is the *new covenant* in *my* blood."

(Pause)

How do the disciples respond as the cup is passed to each of them?

(Pause)

Now, see yourself at the table, reclining next to Jesus. As the unleavened bread is passed, see yourself taking a piece of it. As the cup of red wine is passed, see yourself drinking from it. Look at Jesus and ask him any questions that you have. Perhaps you want to know what this means for your life. What does this *new covenant* mean to you? What does it mean to remember Jesus in the bread and wine? Let yourself ask any question or say anything you want to Jesus. Then, be still and quiet and give him time to respond in some way.

REFLECT
After the prayer, journal your experience with this imaginative prayer.

- What did you experience?
- What impact did this prayer have on you?
- How did this imaginative prayer inform your understanding of

communion?If you are in a group, the facilitator will lead small group or large group sharing. If you are doing this study alone, consider creating a piece of poetry or art depicting your experience.

CONNECTING HOLY COMMUNION WITH OUR LIVES

What happens in this meal with Jesus? In the text, we read that, "Each time we come to the table, we can expect the grace of God to be manifested in a variety of ways."

- We experience how the Holy Spirit makes the presence of Christ come alive in Holy Communion.
- We receive God's gifts of growth, healing, forgiveness, and wholeness.
- We participate in Communion as an act of gratitude. We experience unity by laying aside differences and embodying our fundamental oneness in Christ as we share one loaf and one cup.
- We taste the radical hospitality of Jesus and want all to come to the table and sit in the presence of Jesus.
- We receive the affirmation that love and justice are the will of God. We receive food for our souls, as well as the strength to do the work of caring with others and challenging injustice.
- We experience relationship with Christ.
- We prepare for the larger banquet to come when we participate in Holy Communion.

Think of specific times when you have experienced these gifts of God's grace in the Lord's Supper. Write your memories or share them with another person in the group.

HOLY COMMUNION AND LIFE IN COMMUNITY

In our text we read:

> Paul had invested a year and a half to establish this pioneering community of believers. He instructed these new Jesus followers to be a colony of God within the emperor's colony. They were to be God's alternative to the ways of greed, social climbing, status seeking, and worship of rank and position.
>
> But within a couple of years, Paul learned that this new commonwealth of God was being infected by the prevailing disease. They were dividing into factions, and some were living by the "wisdom of the world" instead of the "wisdom of God."
>
> This disease, Paul learned, was even infecting the Lord's Supper. At that time, the sacred ceremony was genuinely a full meal, a kind of church potluck. Because of an ongoing famine, some of the poorer congregants counted on the common meal to stave off starvation. But the better nourished were getting to the house church earlier than the workers, peasants, and slaves and were eating up the food and drink. Some were even getting drunk (1 Corinthians 11:17–34). (p. 20–21)

Read: 1 Corinthians 11:27–30

How do you respond to Paul's harsh words? Do you want to say anything back to him? What new insight does this offer for you in your community today?

Think about what you just shared regarding the times you received growth, healing, radical hospitality, or other gifts from the list above in Holy Communion. Also think about Paul's words to the Corinthians and call to mind those who are not at the table in your church and in the homes of your neighborhood. When are we like the Corinthians Paul is addressing, in our churches and other areas of our lives? Where do you see the diseases of division, fear, greed, and exclusion at the tables of your life?

Write your responses or share in groups of two or three.

CONNECTING OUR BAPTISMAL COVENANT AND HOLY COMMUNION TO WALKING JUSTLY

What is the connection between our baptismal covenant, having supper in community in communion with Jesus, and walking justly? In the text, we read:

> All the gifts of God are to be shared with all the people of God.
>
> When you participate in Holy Communion, reaffirm to yourself that love and justice are the way and will of God. Even if it is painful, open your eyes to the ways of the world that benefit some people and leave so many on the margins. Remember, too, the systemic destruction of the natural world that is occurring. Ask God to make clear what your part in loving the world is. (p. 25)

Let us reflect on what we have experienced so far in this study. Remember your experience of being God's beloved in baptism, recall the covenant you made with God at the end of Session 1, and consider the gifts of communing with Christ and community in Holy Communion. Now, write a paragraph, poem, or create a piece of art that represents your understanding at this moment of what it means to live sacramentally and walk justly.

CLOSING LITANY (IN UNISON)

O most gracious God, thank you for naming and claiming us as yours; thank you for nurturing and sustaining us always. Grace us with all that we need to be ever more open to your presence at the Communion Table.

May we rush to the table to be with you, to be made whole, to experience unity and inclusive community, to be reminded of your loving communion with all, to say thank you, and to be strengthened for our walk in justice. In Jesus' name we pray, Amen.

HOMEWORK
Read Chapters 2 and 4 for the next session.

Session 3

Answering the Call Part 1: Living Each Day with God

INTRODUCTION

This session is based on chapter 2 and 4 in the text.

> [John] Wesley was a methodical person—so much so that his detractors nicknamed him a "methodist." But Wesley embraced the epithet, and he nurtured followers, showing them a method for accessing God's grace and the Christian life. He called these the "works of piety" and the "works of mercy." These are reliable disciplines through which we receive the "grace sufficient" to meet the challenge to walk faithfully and justly. (p. 37)

This session provides spiritual tools for living out "works of piety." Session 4 will offer spiritual tools for discerning the "works of mercy" God is calling us to at this point in our lives.

GATHERING

ONE VOICE: God calls us to the better part.

MANY VOICES: God wants to be with us. Let us spend time with God.

ONE VOICE: God calls us to the better part.

MANY VOICES: God wants us to grow in God's love. Let us share our experience of God with one another in spiritual friendship.

ONE VOICE: God calls us to the better part.

MANY VOICES: God wants to nourish us. Let us worship and receive Holy Communion.

ONE VOICE: God calls us to the better part.

MANY VOICES: God wants us to be for the world the body of Christ. Let us declare God's kin-dom in word and deed. Let us deepen our understanding of God's ways, revealed through scripture.

One Voice: God calls us to the better part.

MANY VOICES: God wants us to experience God's constant showering of love. Let us fast from our distractions.

ALL VOICES: Let us choose the better part and experience God's abundant grace.

SONG

Come and Find the Quiet Center (*The Faith We Sing*, no. 2128)

OPENING PRAYER

O God of unlimited grace, we thank you for calling us to live our lives in constant awareness of your love and grace. Through this study, help us to grow in our commitment to the means of grace offered through prayer, scripture, Christian conferencing and conversation, fasting, worship, and Holy Communion. Through our faithful practice, may we come to know the joy of living consciously in your ever-present love. Let our lives become a sacrament and give evidence of your presence with us. In Jesus' name we pray, Amen.

HOW TO READ SCRIPTURE

In Chapter 2 of our text, Norberg and McClain make some suggestions for taking scripture to heart. Look at the questions that follow then reflect, and if in a group, discuss how such questions can enrich, and even correct, some scriptural understandings that the church currently has or has had in the past. Keep these questions in your heart as you meditate on the story of Mary and Martha.

SCRIPTURE STUDY: THE BETTER PART, LUKE 10:38–42
We are going to enter a time of prayer through scripture. Before we begin, pause to ask God to shape your prayer and to help you to be open to receive what God wants for you.

(Pause for one minute.)

Read aloud or listen to someone slowly read Jesus' story about "the better part" three times (Luke 10:38–42). Now, to paraphrase our text, sink down into the truest part of yourself—to that place where you are naked, honest, and thirsty. Be quiet and rest for a moment. Let your mind be still, thinking about nothing except resting in God's presence.

> Now as they went on their way, he entered a certain village, where a woman named Martha welcomed him into her home. She had a sister named Mary, who sat at the Lord's feet and listened to what he was saying. But Martha was distracted by her many tasks; so she came to him and asked, "Lord, do you not care that my sister has left me to do all the work by myself? Tell her then to help me." But the Lord answered her, "Martha, Martha, you are worried and distracted by many things; there is need of only one thing. Mary has chosen the better part, which will not be taken away from her."

(Pause for two minutes.)

Let thoughts or images come to you. If they do, notice their qualities. Are they about confession? Praise? Inquiry?

(Pause for a minute.)

Maybe no words or images come. Instead, perhaps there is a sense of peace and contentment, a welcoming into the presence of God. It could be a simple invitation to be still and let God love you.

(Pause for three minutes.)

Let the feelings come. Notice what you are feeling. Are they feelings of doubt? Fear? Rage? Sadness? Emptiness? Love? Peace? Something else? How would you name what you are feeling?

(Pause for three minutes.)

Whatever the feelings are, acknowledge them and let them be. God can speak to us through our feelings. Simply notice what you are feeling and what God is revealing to you.

(Pause for three minutes.)

Notice what happens next. Does a memory surface? Does the image of a person come to mind? Do you feel a nudge to do something—make a phone call, send an e-mail, tell someone something, or take some other action?

(Pause for three minutes.)

Sometimes God speaks to us by urging us to do something. Ask God to make you aware if there is something important you need to do. If there is, double-check with God and ask for affirmation.

REFLECT

After your prayer, ask yourself:

- Was my prayer full of God or full of me?
- Am I expecting or insisting my prayer to be answered a particular way, or am I open to something new God is doing in me?
- Ask God to keep showing you what is from God. Trust that God will honor your desire to hear and do as God desires.

(Pause for three minutes.)

As you write in a journal or create a piece of art, consider the feelings, thoughts, questions, answers, and insights that have come to you during this prayer time. Also consider the thanks you want to give to God, as well as the areas you want to ask God to continue to help you change, heal, and grow.

Sometimes, there is discomfort or confusion in prayer. You may not know what is really going on or what to ask for. Or perhaps you don't feel gratitude for anything. If so, feel free to simply ask God by writing in the journal or creating art that expresses, "Please help me!"

LIFE DISCIPLINE

We have looked at the works of piety that open the window to means of grace in the study sessions: Holy Communion, worship, scripture, prayer, Christian conferencing and conversation, and fasting. These works help us live life as a sacrament and aware of God's presence.

Consider each of the works of piety and how you want to commit to them. This is called a "Life Discipline." A Life Discipline sets out the works of piety that you want to commit to daily, weekly, monthly, and annually. For instance, some people commit to daily spiritual or scripture reading, prayer or meditation, or journaling; weekly Sabbath-keeping, worship, Holy Communion; weekly or monthly Christian conferencing; monthly fasting; and an annual spiritual retreat. You can set out your plans in a Life Discipline and update it on a regular basis (annually), or as you feel God's urging to do so.

Take some time now to consider what works of piety you want to practice and begin forming your Life Discipline. A Life Discipline leads to and supports works of mercy. Consider the following questions and suggestions as your consider what your Life Discipline will be:

- ■ Holy Communion and worship: How often do you want to commit to practicing these and how do you want to experience them? Daily? Weekly? Do you want to seek out new worship or Communion experiences on a planned basis?

- ■ Prayer: How often do you want to commit to spending time in prayer? How long each day? What prayer practice do you want to explore? *Lectio divina,* imaginative prayer with scripture, or another form of spiritual reading and meditation?

- ■ Christian conferencing and conversation: Do you want to commit to meeting with a spiritual friend or a group of spiritual friends? Do you plan to participate in spiritual sharing during United Methodist Women gatherings or another church meeting? How often should you meet?

- ■ Fasting: When do you plan to fast? Will it be a fast from food or something else in your life to strengthen your connection and openness to the presence of God?

Works of mercy: Works of mercy are the result of our connecting more and more with God through works of piety. They are also spiritual practice, facilitating our connection with God. As spiritual practice, works of mercy increase our ability to be a vessel of God's love to put us in touch with our belovedness, with God's grace and with others in community. In the next session, we will focus on how to continue to discern God's call in our lives. Notice now if there's a work of mercy that has been on your mind and your heart. To help you think about works of mercy, look at this list of possibilities from Brian McLaren's book *Finding Our Way Again:*

- ■ Forgiving those who wrong us.
- ■ Showing hospitality to strangers—or "the other."
- ■ Praying for the sick.
- ■ Not judging but showing mercy and compassion.
- ■ Confronting evil, seeking to overcome it with good.
- ■ Serving.
- ■ Listening.

- Associating with the [marginalized].
- Giving "the holy kiss" [eating with marginalized].
- Speaking truth in love.
- Practicing neighborliness, including toward enemies.
- Preferring the poor rather than showing favoritism to the rich.
- Speaking and working for justice.
- Proclaiming the good news in word and deed.
- Giving to the poor.
- Throwing parties for poor and forgotten.
- Walking to the other side of the street to serve those in need.
- Showing empathy.[1]

MAKING YOUR LIFE DISCIPLINE

Now we invite you to write your Life Discipline. Choose the works of piety that you are ready to commit to on a daily, weekly, monthly, and/or yearly time frame. Be realistic about how any new time commitment will work into your life. Periodically, such as on your birthday or for New Year's, review, affirm and update your Life Discipline as needed.

Take a moment to place yourself in God's presence and ask for guidance as you choose the spiritual practices for your Life Discipline.

You may use a journal or worksheet in the appendix on page 175.

Daily practice: Choose the time of day you will pray, read, journal; where you will go for your prayer period (e.g., a corner of a room, a favorite chair, a place outdoors); what resource you will use for the reading; what method of prayer (e.g., *lectio divina*, imaginative prayer, silent meditation, intercessory, contemplation of the passage); whether you will journal, create art, or identify some other outlet to process your prayer time.

Weekly practice: Your weekly practices may include worship, Holy

Communion, Christian conferencing, fasting, or Sabbath-keeping (spending a day enjoying God through time in nature, with family and friends, reading, walking, etc.).

Monthly practice: Possibilities for your monthly practice could include Holy Communion, fasting, meeting with a spiritual director, Christian conferencing, and a day set aside to be with God.

Annual practice: If you plan to have an annual spiritual retreat, set aside three to eight days to spend time alone with God, either guided by a spiritual director or a retreat leader. If your local, district, or conference United Methodist Women has an annual or biannual spiritual day apart, plan to attend it. The Upper Room offers several opportunities for annual retreats, including the Academy for Spiritual Formation and SOULfeast (www.upperroom.org.) Contact retreat centers in your area or an area you'd like to visit.

Commitment: Changes in lifestyle are not easy or convenient. Think about how you can make it possible to incorporate your Life Discipline into your life. Would it help to put your daily prayer time and weekly commitments on your calendar? Would it be helpful to schedule next year's annual retreat? Be specific in naming what you need to do to be skillful at keeping this commitment.

CLOSING

Offering Your Life Discipline to God (in unison)

O God of unlimited grace, thank you for showing us the works of piety that open us to your means of grace. We need your grace even to stay faithful to the works of piety we commit to now. And we do commit to these spiritual practices, to the better part.

(Hold your Life Discipline in the silence with God.)

Bless our intentions as we dedicate time to be with you daily, weekly, monthly, and annually, so that we can live sacramentally, as evidence of your love, and walk justly in your loving kin-dom. In Jesus' name, Amen.

HOMEWORK

Read Chapters 3 and 5 in preparation for Session 4.

---

1   Brian McLaren, *Finding our Way Again: The Return of the Ancient Practices* (Nashville: Thomas Nelson, 2008), 119.

Session 4

Answering the Call Part 2: Following Jesus in Caring for God's World

INTRODUCTION

Christian discernment rests on the assumption that God does indeed want to communicate, does have a plan for us, that God has claimed us and empowers us for living sacramentally and walking justly. Through discernment, we can begin to sense how, even in our seemingly inconsequential lives, God is still making all things new. We can catch glimpses of God's greatness, as God reveals God's self to us. . . . (p. 77)

Our commitment to practicing the works of piety in our Life Discipline helps us to live Wesley's teaching about the means of grace. As we seek to live sacramentally, we also acknowledge Wesley's teaching that the only holiness is social holiness and we work to deepen our understanding of how God calls us to walk justly.

In this session, we will contemplate God's actions in a call story from scripture, call stories of others in our time, and learn spiritual tools to help us discern and affirm our call to walk justly.

GATHERING

ONE VOICE: Jesus calls us to follow the path he walked: living sacramentally, walking justly.

MANY VOICES: **But how do I know what God wants me to *do*? How do I know God is calling me to "walk justly?" What does it mean *for me* to walk justly?**

ONE VOICE: Jesus calls us and Jesus will show us the way.

MANY VOICES: **I am ready to watch and learn and listen. Who do I watch? Who do I learn from? Who do I listen to?**

ONE VOICE: Ourselves, each other, God.

MANY VOICES: **I am ready to watch, to learn, to listen, to discern God's call for me.**

ALL VOICES: **Let us study together.**

SONG

Lord, You Have Come to the Lakeshore (*The United Methodist Hymnal*, no. 344)

PRAYER (IN UNISON)

O God of astounding hope, you call us to help you bring your kin-dom to completion. We are always amazed, and sometimes perplexed by your ways. And we are increasingly willing to help you. We come now to learn the ways of discernment so that we can walk with you each day. We want to answer your specific call to each of us to give our lives for the world that you have created. We want to live so we may all share in your love and justice. In Jesus' name, we pray, Amen.

SCRIPTURE STUDY—THE BOOK OF JONAH

In Chapter 3, McClain and Norberg remind us that, "God calls each of us to join the healing stream of God's love and justice, and our baptism is the symbol of that call. But how exactly does God call?" How do we recognize God's calling? One way is through stories. The study provides numerous examples from the Bible and from the lives of historical and modern-day people. Let's take a fresh look at a familiar story from the Bible that many of us first heard during our childhood—the story of Jonah.

Read the Book of Jonah individually or listen as it is read in the group.

REFLECT

Individually, or in small groups, consider and share your thoughts about some of the following questions:

Jonah's story

- What do you find most interesting in this story?
- How would you characterize Jonah and God's relationship?
- Why do you think Jonah doesn't want to answer God's call?
- Does God give up on calling Jonah?
- How does God stay in relationship with Jonah?
- How does God work with Jonah? Is there a pattern in the way God calls Jonah?
- How does Jonah know what God is doing with him; that it's God calling and engaging him?

Connecting Jonah's story to our story.

■ Do you identify with Jonah? In what way?

■ What are the reasons we don't want to do what we think God might be asking of us?

■ Have you ever turned the other way or been silent and not responded to something you felt God was calling you to do?

EXPLORING CALL STORIES

As McClain and Norberg explain in Chapter 3, "The biblical accounts of God's call are perhaps the most familiar, but God has never stopped finding unlikely times and places to call us by name." Let us explore call stories.

Review the story of how Maggie Liechty (p. 75) received a call, as McClain and Norberg put it, "in the crucible of her own great weakness and suffering." Discuss in twos or threes how you may have received God's call in the "crucible of [your] own great weakness and suffering." Reflect on additional stories you connect to in Chapter 4, or the stories of others you know.

TOOL FOR DAILY DISCERNMENT: THE DAILY EXAMEN

"Openness to God's prompting on a daily—even hourly— basis can lead to a lively ongoing conversation with God. Discernment can enable us to order our lives in accordance with God's invitation to live sacramentally" (p. 77).

In their helpful discussion of discernment in Chapter 3, McClain and Norberg offer several questions to consider in our lifelong process of discernment.

The Daily Examen is another spiritual tool in the Christian tradition that helps us in this process. As we practice it each day (it only takes ten minutes), we can see a pattern in our lives. It's a daily check-in to see how we're doing with our call, if God is tweaking our call, or calling us in some other direction.

To practice the Daily Examen, set aside ten minutes at the end of the day to ask God to bring to your mind the answers to two questions (please feel free to adapt the questions as needed):

1. When did I most contribute love and justice to God's kin-dom today? Make note of the answer and give thanks to God.

2. When did I least contribute love and justice to God's kin-dom today? Make note of the answer and ask God to help you.

You may choose to journal the answer to both questions. This tool helps discern God's desires for you, as over weeks and months, you notice a pattern in the answers.[1]

THE CALL TO LOVE AND JUSTICE

As we remember the covenant of our baptism and God's sustaining love in Holy Communion, we commit to living sacramentally through the disciplines of spiritual practice, and that leads us to action.

We are called as individuals and we are called as Christian community to bring love and justice. God's call to action on our individual lives is to be accomplished in community. In Chapter 3, McClain and Norberg give examples of United Methodist churches and groups that are working toward making systemic changes such as intercepting human trafficking, engaging in community conversations, and advocating for state legislation that will benefit "the least among us."

United Methodist Women members join together locally, nationally, and globally in various forms of prayer to create change. They are keeping vigil for the DREAMers, children brought to this country illegally and who now are in college. The DREAM Act would give them a path to citizenship. As part of their witness, a group of people fast and pray each day for the DREAMers.[2]

The author of Ephesians writes about the necessity of confronting unjust systems: "For our struggle is not against enemies of blood and flesh, but against the rulers, against the authorities, against the cosmic powers of this present darkness, against the spiritual forces of evil in the heavenly places" (Ephesians 6:11–12).

Prayer is one form of community activism. In a public space, it can be a transforming testimony. Many believe that years of peace prayers offered every Monday night in a church in Leipzig, Germany, resulted in the fall of the Berlin Wall.

Consider the women of Liberia who brought peace to their country after years of civil war. Leymah Gbowee, a thirty-nine-year-old Lutheran mother of six and Liberian peace activist, showed Christian and Muslim women how to break down the stereotypes so that they could find common goals to work for peace in their country.

In 2003, after years of civil war, she called these women of faith in Liberia to peace building, and they established a public witness of prayer for peace. The women's movement eventually led to the ousting of President Charles Taylor and the election of Ellen Johnson Sirleaf, with whom Gbowee said she has a "mother–daughter relationship."

President Johnson Sirleaf is a United Methodist and the first female to be elected a head of state in modern Africa. Gbowee's struggle for peace in Liberia is documented in her memoir *Mighty Be Our Powers: How Sisterhood, Prayer, and Sex Changes a Nation at War* and the documentary "Pray the Devil Back to Hell."[3]

WRITING YOUR OBITUARY

Imagine that you are coming to the end of a long and fruitful life and that it is time to write your obituary. This obituary is a little different from the ones you read in the newspaper. It is a review of how you answered God's call to be love and do justice in the world. It should list the ways you have helped others, the people you loved, and the actions you took with your community to address injustice and bring about systemic change. It contains the ways you helped bring God's kin-dom further into completion. Let your heart lead you in writing this obituary. Write with the passion and urgency for the "least of these" or the injustice in the world that you most want to see changed. Let this obituary record what you hope your life will accomplish, from this moment on.

Now, compare this obituary with where you are in your life right now. Are you taking the necessary actions to accomplish these goals?

If you are in a group setting, gather into small groups and share your obituaries. Then, consider making a plan together to join around one issue of injustice and decide how you will organize a prayer vigil for this change. How often will you come together to pray? Where will you pray? If it's in a public space, what is the best place to bring awareness to this issue? What are the elements of the prayer that you want to include: fasting, song, silence, candles, walking, signs, artwork, words? How long will you continue to pray? With whom can you combine forces to help make a difference? Imagine what your goal is and the steps necessary for change to take place.

While it's fresh in your mind, prayerfully transfer the hopes for your life written in your obituary into a covenant and make a promise to God to take action in one area of injustice or one system in need of change.

LOVE FEAST

Prepare now to share in a Love Feast,[4] a special expression of deep Christian   fellowship rooted in the Methodist tradition extending back to John Wesley's experience with the Moravians who introduced the feast to him. Through sharing stories about how we perceive God in our lives, singing, and sharing food, the Love Feast is marked by the tenderness of enjoying community as the family of Christ.

There is no strict structure to the Love Feast. It is a Spirit-led time of prayer in which participants are invited to share impromptu readings of scripture passages, give personal witness, pass a plate and cup of simple food and drink, and sing songs, chosen spontaneously.

One suggestion is to begin with singing "Here I Am, Lord," which points to God's call to serve and witness and to our heart's response.[5]

Food is shared quietly, without interrupting the flow of the service. It is merely passed as the other sharing proceeds. (To distinguish this liturgy from Holy Communion, food other than bread and grape juice are shared—for instance, a cracker and apple juice.)

During the final sharing time in this Love Feast, participants are invited to talk about how you have felt God calling during this study and how you are committing to social justice.

A suggested closing is to prayerfully recite together the words to the hymn "God of Grace and God of Glory."[6]

---

1 Dennis Linn, Sheila Fabricant Linn, Matthew Linn, *Sleeping with Bread. Holding What Gives You Life* (Mahwah/New York: Paulist Press, 1995), 7.

2 See www.facebook.com/groups/176134225738078/.

3 Linda Bloom, "Peace prize winner shines her light," (New York: United Methodist News Service, 2010).

4 *The United Methodist Book of Worship* (Nashville: The United Methodist Publishing House, 1992), 581.

5 "Here I am, Lord," *The United Methodist Hymnal* (Nashville, Abingdon Press, 1993), 593.

6 "God of Grace and God of Glory," *The United Methodist Hymnal,* 577.

Bibliography

Bloom, Linda. "Peace prize winner shines her light." United Methodist News Service, October 10, 2011. www.umc.org/site/apps/nlnet/content3.aspx?c=lwL4KnN1LtH&b=5259669&ct=11288921.

Gbowee, Leymah. *Mighty Be Our Powers: How Sisterhood, Prayer, and Sex Changes a Nation at War.* New York: Beast Books, 2011.

Linn, Dennis, Sheila Fabricant Linn, and Matthew Linn. *Sleeping with Bread. Holding What Gives You Life.* Mahwah, NJ: Paulist Press, 1995.

McLaren, Brian. *Finding our Way Again: The Return of the Ancient Practices.* Nashville: Thomas Nelson, 2008.

Nouwen, Henri. *Life of the Beloved: Spiritual Living in a Secular World.* New York: Crossroad, 1992.

Pray the Devil Back to Hell. Directed by Gini Reticker. New York: Fork Films, 2008.

The United Methodist Book of Worship. Nashville: The United Methodist Publishing House, 1992.

The United Methodist Hymnal. Nashville: The United Methodist Publishing House, 1989.

About the Editor

Nancy Kruh, who also wrote Chapters 4 and 5, is a freelance editor and writer based in Nashville who worked for twenty-three years as an editor and features staff writer at *The Dallas Morning News*. She is also the author of *The Disciple Story: The Transforming Power of Scripture* and editor/co-author of *This I Know* (www.thisiknowstudy.org).

Kruh's editing and writing has earned her numerous state and national awards, including the Barbara Jordan Award, the Women's Sports Foundation Journalism Award, the Austin (Texas) Headliners Club Award, the Texas Associated Press Managing Editors Award, and the Texas Daily Newspaper Association's John Murphy Award.

Contributors

George McClain has been involved in a ministry of social justice and spiritual formation since participating in the historic Selma-to-Montgomery March of 1965. After serving on an interracial team with the Methodist Student Movement and co-pastoring a church with his wife, Tilda Norberg, on Staten Island, New York, McClain served as the executive director of the Methodist Federation for Social Action for twenty-five years.

McClain later founded a prison theological education program in which he, Norberg, and other church volunteers taught for fourteen years. His doctoral work was published as *Claiming All Things for God: Prayer, Discernment, and Ritual for Social Change.* Through New York Seminary and United Methodist Women, McClain teaches mission theology and United Methodist studies to prospective deaconesses and home missioners.

Tilda Norberg has spent over forty years counseling and training hundreds of counselors, social workers, lay ministers, and clergy in Gestalt Pastoral Care (GPC), which she created. GPC is a unique blend of Gestalt work, healing prayer, and spiritual companionship. She has worked with clergy and laity in retreat settings, private practice, and the Gestalt Pastoral Care (www.gestaltpastoralcare.com) training program, which was founded in 1985.

Norberg is the author of the basic GPC text, *Consenting to Grace: An Introduction to Gestalt Pastoral Care,* as well as co-author of *Stretch Out Your Hand: Exploring Healing Prayer,* and author of *Ashes Transformed: Healing from Trauma; Gathered Together: Creating Personal Liturgies for Heal-*

ing and Transformation; and *The Chocolate-Covered Umbrella: Discovering Your Dreamcode.* Her first book, *Threadbear, A Story of Christian Healing for Adult Survivors of Sexual Abuse* was published by Penn House Press.

Pat Hoerth is a deaconess in The United Methodist Church. She serves as spiritual director and retreat leader at Turtle Rock Farm, a center for sustainability, spirituality, and healing, which is located in north central Oklahoma. A former staff writer for *The Washington Star,* Hoerth writes the daily blog www.turtlerockfarm.wordpress.com to encourage attentiveness to God's good creation and learning to live sustainably.

Previously, Hoerth compiled and edited the stories and recipes of Oklahoma cooks for the Oklahoma Folklife Council and co-authored *The Life and Times of Henry Bellmon.*

Becky Dodson Louter is a United Methodist deaconess serving as the executive for the program office that administers the Offices of Deaconess, Home Missioner, and Home Missionary. She is based in both New York City and Johnson City, Tennessee.

Previously, Louter coordinated a recruitment, education, and crisis support network for foster and adoptive families in Kentucky. Her career also has included work at a United Methodist retirement community and a United Methodist-affiliated college.

Worksheet for Creating a Life Discipline

MY PRACTICES

(e.g., Scripture reading, spiritual reading, Daily Examen, meditation, centering prayer, retreat, Christian conferencing, Holy Communion, fasting, seeing a spiritual director, worship, works of mercy, etc.)

I commit to the following practices:

<u>Daily:</u>

_____

_____

_____

_____

_____

_____

_____

_____

_____

Weekly:

_____

_____

_____

_____

_____

_____

_____

_____

_____

_____

_____

_____

Monthly:

_____

_____

_____

_____

_____

_____

_____

_____

_____

_____

_____

_____

_____

_____

_____

<u>Annually:</u>

_____
_____
_____
_____
_____
_____
_____
_____
_____
_____
_____
_____
_____

WORKS OF MERCY

Works of mercy are the result of our connecting more and more with God through works of piety and they are also spiritual practice, facilitating our connection with God.

I commit to the following works of mercy:

_____
_____
_____
_____
_____
_____
_____
_____

SCHEDULING YOUR LIFE DISCIPLINE

What needs to change in my schedule to make room for the Life Discipline practices I am committing to?

_____

_____

_____

_____

What additions and planning steps do I need to make? (e.g., scheduling of annual retreat, deciding on a regular time period to review the Life Discipline, such as on my birthday, etc.)

_____

_____

_____

_____

WHAT DO I NEED TO DO TO MAKE TIME FOR THESE PRACTICES?

<u>Daily:</u>

_____

_____

_____

_____

_____

<u>Weekly:</u>

_____

_____

_____

_____

Monthly:

_____
_____
_____
_____
_____
_____
_____
_____
_____
_____
_____
_____
_____
_____

Annually:

_____
_____
_____
_____
_____
_____
_____
_____
_____
_____
_____
_____
_____
_____
_____
_____

ALSO AVAILABLE:

Spanish translation of *The Call: Living Sacramentally, Walking Justly* by George McClain, Tilda Norberg, and Nancy Kruh (Editor)
ISBN: 978-0-9885612-0-5
M3124-2013-01
$7.00

Korean translation of *The Call: Living Sacramentally, Walking Justly* George McClain, Tilda Norberg, and Nancy Kruh (Editor)
ISBN: 978-0-9885612-1-2
M3125-2013-01
$7.00

response magazine, April 2013 issue focusing on answering the call to follow Christ

Place your order with:
United Methodist Women Mission Resources
1-800-305-9857
www.umwmissionresources.org

The Call: Living Sacramentally, Walking Justly webpage:
www.unitedmethodistwomen.org/thecall